# Regulatory Reform in Air Cargo Transportation

## Lucile Sheppard Keyes

American Enterprise Institute for Public Policy Research
Washington, D.C.

**Library of Congress Cataloging in Publication Data**

Keyes, Lucile Sheppard.
　　Regulatory reform in air cargo transportation.

　　(Studies in government regulation) (AEI studies ;
268)
　　　　1. Aeronautics, Commercial—United States—Freight.
2. Aeronautics, Commercial—Law and legislation—
United States. I. Title. II. Series. III. Series:
American Enterprise Institute for Public Policy
Research. AEI studies ; 268.
KF2447.K49　　　　343.73'0978　　　　79-26666
ISBN 0-8447-3371-7

AEI Studies 268

*Printed in the United States of America*

# CONTENTS

# INTRODUCTION

With the signing of H.R. 6010 on November 9, 1977, a system of federal economic regulation of domestic air cargo transportation which had existed for nearly forty years was almost totally dismantled. For most of the industry, the reform became effective immediately; for the rest, the effective date was one year after the date of enactment. At the time of passage, only about nineteen months had elapsed since drastic liberalization of air cargo regulation had first been recommended by an official governmental source. Government-sponsored proposals for basic reform of the regulation of surface transportation have a much longer history but have so far met with relatively little success, and the reform of air passenger transport regulation, which was being considered concurrently with the cargo measure, appeared to be only a remote possibility at the time the latter was approved. The circumstances accounting for the subsequent success of "deregulation" on the passenger side will be discussed in Chapter 4.

What made this remarkable development possible? Had the preexisting regulatory framework produced economically undesirable effects which became obvious to all concerned? What were the origins of the reform and what principal influences were at work in the formulation and adoption of the final legislation? What does early experience under the law indicate regarding the actual results of its passage? And, finally, is any of this experience relevant to the reform of regulation in other fields? It is the purpose of this study to suggest some answers to these questions.

Chapter 1 will set forth briefly the major elements of the preexisting regulatory scheme and will present evidence of its economic effects. In Chapter 2 the origins and evolution of the 1977 legislation will be discussed. Some postenactment developments which seem relevant to the future course of regulatory policy and the results to be expected from reform will be taken up in Chapter 3. Chapter 4 will summarize the study and assess the significance of its findings for regulatory reform initiatives in other spheres of economic activity. As a preliminary, the following short introduction to the industry, its terminology, and its major participants should be helpful to readers unfamiliar with the field.

The term "air cargo" encompasses three classes of traffic: air mail, air express, and air freight. (Official air cargo revenue statistics usually also include revenues from passenger baggage in excess of the maximum allowed to be carried without charge.) "Air express" denotes traffic consisting of small parcels moving on a priority basis at relatively high rates, while "air freight" denotes larger, heavier shipments carried at lower rates. Together, these two classes of cargo are referred to as "property." For many years air freight has been the dominant component of air cargo, by 1976 accounting for almost 80 percent of the total domestic scheduled cargo revenue ton-miles.[1]

The major airlines, both trunkline and local service, are authorized to carry both passengers and cargo; they are therefore sometimes called combination carriers or combination airlines. The all-cargo airlines (for example, the Flying Tiger Line, Seaboard World Airlines, and Airlift International) carry cargo only (with some unimportant exceptions) in all-cargo aircraft known as "freighters." Combination carriers transport air cargo in freighters as well as in the lower compartments (bellies) of passenger-carrying aircraft. In recent years, commuter airlines (carriers providing scheduled air transportation in small aircraft) have provided a minor but rapidly growing source of air cargo transportation.

The trunk airlines have always been and continue to be the major carriers of domestic air cargo, although their share of total scheduled revenue ton-miles declined from 86.9 percent in 1969 to

---

[1] Douglas V. Leister and Bruce N. Stram, "Vertical Integration, Intermodality, and the Public Interest Through 'Deregulation' of the Domestic Air Cargo Industry," in *Research Frontiers in Marketing: Dialogues and Directions*, Subhash C. Jain, ed. (Chicago: American Marketing Association, 1978), pp. 244–248. The present writer is indebted to the authors of this very informative article for access to the work in manuscript form. Their statistical analysis was based on reports to the Civil Aeronautics Board by the carriers.

81.9 percent in 1977;[2] however, less than 10 percent of combination carrier revenues has come from air cargo transportation.[3]

Though more than half of air cargo traffic has continued to move in passenger-carrying aircraft,[4] freighter airlift is of special value to a large proportion of shippers. Service by passenger-carrying planes has the major disadvantage of being scheduled almost entirely during the daylight hours to accommodate passenger demand. Freighter aircraft are normally flown at night, so that service can be available for shipments ready at or near the end of the working day in time to provide next-morning delivery at their intended destinations. Ready availability of transportation obviously reduces the need for costly additional handling and storage. In addition, freighters are able to accommodate large-size shipments and are considered by some shippers to be more reliable in ensuring proper handling and priority treatment.[5]

Most shippers of air freight prefer to purchase air transportation as part of a total package including pickup and delivery and in some cases supervision of in-transit transfers and consolidation of small shipments into larger ones which move at lower per-pound rates. The scheduled airlines provide pickup and delivery through a wholly owned subsidiary, Air Cargo, Inc., which uses a large number of trucking firms serving airports throughout the country. Alongside this service by the *direct air carriers*,[6] a specialized air freight forwarder industry has grown and prospered. These forwarders, which are classified as *indirect carriers*,[7] provide a full complement of surface transportation and related services to air freight shippers and are an important source of airline traffic. In 1977 it was estimated that be-

---

[2] Ibid.

[3] Civil Aeronautics Board, *Reports to Congress*, Fiscal Year 1977 and Transitional Quarter.

[4] Leister and Stram, "Vertical Integration."

[5] *Domestic Air Freight Rate Investigation* (Docket 22859), *Initial Decision of the Administrative Law Judge* (1975), pp. 37–38.

[6] The term "direct air carrier" is defined by the Civil Aeronautics Board (CAB) in its *Glossary of Air Transportation Terms* (February 1977) as: "Any air carrier directly engaged in operation of aircraft, pursuant to a certificate of public convenience and necessity issued under . . . the Federal Aviation Act of 1958, as amended, or under the authority conferred by any applicable regulation or order of the Board."

[7] In the CAB *Glossary* the term "indirect air carrier" is defined as: "Any citizen of the United States who engages indirectly in air transportation including air freight forwarders, persons authorized by the Board to transport by air used household goods of personnel of the Department of Defense, tour operators, study group charterers, overseas military personnel charter operators, and travel group charter organizers."

tween 40 and 45 percent of the freight volume of the scheduled air carriers was generated by forwarders.[8]

The air cargo industry, although accounting for a very small proportion of the total market for intercity transportation of property in this country,[9] performs a vital service for shippers of such products as perishables, other items with very rapid obsolescence (for example, clothing and publications), and a broad range of products, including medical supplies and spare parts, which fill emergency needs. Though the cost of air transport generally greatly exceeds that of surface transportation, use of air cargo transportation frequently engenders savings in nontransport expenses, such as inventory costs, which more than offset the higher price.

---

[8] U.S. Congress, Senate, Subcommittee on Aviation of the Committee on Commerce, Science, and Transportation, *Hearings on Regulatory Reform in Air Transportation*, 95th Congress, 1st Session, 1977, p. 1115.

[9] In each of the years 1973–1977, inclusive, air cargo represented about 0.18 percent of U.S. total ton-miles of intercity property transportation.

# 1

# Effects of Economic Regulation on Industry Development before Passage of the Reform Legislation

All the participants in the air cargo industry—direct air carriers, air freight forwarders, and various types of surface carriers—have been subject to control over operating authority by the Civil Aeronautics Board (CAB) or the Interstate Commerce Commission (ICC). They have also been subject, in varying degrees, to price regulation by these agencies. Many other operations and transactions of these companies have been federally regulated, but controls over entry and pricing have been of primary importance in shaping the industry; the following discussion deals with these forms of control. The first section of this chapter will briefly outline federal controls over operating authority and pricing as they existed before the air cargo regulatory reform legislation was enacted. In the second section, some important economic effects of these controls will be identified.

## Prereform Regulation of Operating Authority and Pricing

**Air Carrier Participation in Air Transportation.** Under the Federal Aviation Act of 1958, which until very recently contained substantially the same set of provisions regarding economic regulation of air carriers as had been in force since 1938 under the Civil Aeronautics Act, participation in common carrier interstate air transportation requires CAB authorization either by a certificate of public convenience and necessity or by administrative exemption. Thus, certificates specifying the routes to be served, and often containing additional limitations on authority, define the legal operations of the trunkline and local service air carriers. Before the reform legislation, certificated all-cargo carriers were also confined to specified routes, as well as being almost exclusively limited to the carriage of cargo rather than passengers. For both types of carriers, therefore, the geographical scope of the authority was narrowly specified, with the exception of a very limited right to provide off-route charter service. The supplemental carriers, although also certified, were not limited to specified routes but were authorized to provide only charter rather than route-type transportation.[1] In addition, they have not been entitled to engage in "split" chartering: that is, an entire aircraft was required to be chartered to one individual, although this individual might, in turn, provide space to others and bill them on the basis of a pro rata share of the charter fee. Direct air carriers operating under the commuter exemption, although free to engage in scheduled service and to carry passengers as well as cargo, were not permitted to utilize aircraft with a payload exceeding 7,500 pounds (a limit which was raised by the CAB to 18,000 pounds shortly before the passage of the air cargo reform legislation). "Private" or "contract" furnishers of direct air transportation may operate without geographic limit and with any size of equipment but are subject to other restrictions on the number of shippers per planeload and the duration of contract arrangements.

Air freight forwarders are not authorized to engage in direct air carriage (that is, they may not own, lease, or operate aircraft without obtaining additional specific authority), although they have since 1948 been allowed to charter in interstate air transportation, and these charters may be obtained from supplemental as well as route-type carriers.[2] Since 1955, "joint loading" of these charters by two or more forwarders has been permitted.[3]

**Air Carrier Participation in Surface Transportation.** Air carrier participation in surface carriage is also strictly limited by regulation. Pickup and delivery (PUD) service by both direct and indirect air

---

[1] The Airline Deregulation Act of 1978 changed the designation of these carriers from "supplemental" carriers to "charter" carriers. To avoid confusion, the earlier "supplemental" designation has been retained throughout this work.

[2] In overseas and foreign air transportation, however, it has been extremely difficult for supplementals to provide charters for forwarders, because of CAB and International Air Transport Association (IATA) regulations. See Civil Aeronautics Board, *Air Freight Forwarders' Charters Investigation*, Order 77-7-25 (1977), p. 1.

[3] Ibid. "Joint loading is a practice in which two or more air freight forwarders assemble their freight under an agreement designating one forwarder as the 'master biller,' or shipper, of all of the freight so collected. This practice enables the joint-loading forwarders to share the lower per-pound cost which may result from the larger shipment. The Board has traditionally permitted forwarders to engage in joint loading both on scheduled flights and on charters, and has required all joint loading agreements to be open, on reasonable and nondiscriminatory conditions, to other forwarders who wish to participate."

carriers has been generally confined to an area within a twenty-five to fifty-mile radius of the point of origin or termination of air carriage by the terms of an agreement arrived at by the CAB and ICC. Until very recently, the PUD zone defined by the agreement specified a twenty-five-mile radius subject to administrative exceptions. In the spring of 1979 this radius was extended to thirty-five miles.

Direct air carriers may also contract with ICC-certified surface carriers to provide pickup and delivery services beyond the PUD zone or to provide substitute service on routes for which the air carriers possess direct air operating authority, but in each case further regulatory requirements have restricted the service which may be offered. In the first case, the surface transportation ordinarily had to be provided at the ICC-specified common-carrier rates, and these rates were generally insufficient to enable truckers to provide the expedited service important to most shippers of freight by air.[4] In the second case, the CAB rules governing substitute service generally still require that it be provided only between points where some air service is being offered and, in addition, only if accompanied by prior or subsequent air movement.[5]

Air freight forwarder participation in surface transportation is generally subject to the same limitations as apply to direct air carriers. There are, however, a number of exceptions—notably United Parcel Service, a large air freight forwarder which has obtained extensive trucking authority from the ICC as a surface freight forwarder.

---

[4] The situation was explained by a Flying Tiger official in Senate Subcommittee on Aviation of the Committee on Commerce, Science, and Transportation, *Regulatory Reform, 1977*, p. 503: "we are severely restricted in our ability to assure a quality of surface movement which our shippers want and are willing to pay for. Bear in mind that the average air freight shipment tendered by a direct shipper is about 50 pounds. While surface carriers provide excellent service for truckload movements, their economics and rates do not support priority scheduling for small shipments. Consequently, unless the volume of air freight customarily available for surface transfer is substantially equivalent to the truckload, we have considerable difficulty in arranging with the surface carrier for the provision of the expedited service. Were we able to contract with the trucker for truckload service and charge shippers appropriately for the higher value of service which they demand, we would be able to improve the utility of our services for many of the smaller and medium sized communities which today do not have a sufficient volume to support expedited freight service by air or truck at the usual surface rates." As will be noted in Chapter 3, this difficulty has been removed by the pricing provisions of the air cargo reform legislation.

[5] Civil Aeronautics Board, *Substitution of Other Services for Air Transportation Rule Proceeding*, Order 75-3-37 (March 12, 1975) summarizes these rules (p. 3). A few exceptions to these rules have been authorized by the CAB in unusual circumstances.

**Surface Carrier Participation in Air Transportation.** Under a very long-standing interpretation of the Federal Aviation Act, the CAB has all but excluded surface carriers from participating in direct air transportation.[6] Such participation is permitted only if the use of aircraft is supplementary and auxiliary to surface carriage and if, in addition, the CAB finds it to be in the public interest. Since 1969, however, intercity surface carriers have been permitted to act as air freight forwarders, and the CAB has recently reconfirmed this decision.[7]

**Reasons for Limits on Operating Authority.** The generally accepted purpose of certification is to protect existing operators from "excessive" competitive inroads on their revenues; some of the operating restrictions described above can also be explained in terms of this aim. The certificates issued to the route-type air carriers are directly designed to stake out territories within which they enjoy protected status, and the additional class-of-traffic limitation on the cargo certificates has provided further protection for the combination carriers. Limitation of the supplemental carriers to charter transportation and of the commuters to small aircraft has ensured that these operations would remain substantially noncompetitive with the certificated carriers. Similarly, confinement of air freight forwarders to indirect air carriage may have deterred them from providing a total transportation service in competition with direct air carriers as well as ensured that these carriers would not be at a disadvantage in competing for traffic handled by forwarders.

The reluctance of the ICC to grant air carriers extensive automatic surface operating rights beyond the PUD zone is understandable in view of that agency's undeniable duty to regulate entry into

---

[6] See *American President Lines*, et al., *Petition*, 7 CAB 799 (1947).

[7] Alfred E. Kahn, chairman, CAB, "Air Freight Forwarding in an Era of Regulatory Reform," presentation at the Annual Spring Meeting of the Air Freight Forwarders Association of America, Washington, D.C., June 2, 1978, p. 12 (mimeographed): "Way back in 1969 . . . the Board for the first time permitted long-haul surface carriers to go into the air freight forwarding business. More recently we looked at the experience under that ruling, and found that none of the predicted evils had materialized. The integrated carriers had not impaired the ability of independent forwarders to compete; nor had our ruling resulted in a diversion of traffic from air to surface—it was originally argued that truckers controlling air freight forwarders would not have an incentive to develop the air cargo business, but would instead divert freight to their surface fleets. On the contrary, while the effect of our decision was apparently not great, it had, we found, encouraged new competitive challenges—helped bring new services to outlying areas, and helped generally to promote air transport."

surface transportation. Similarly, the ICC's duty to regulate surface rates can be cited to justify its insistence that truckers under contract to air carriers charge only the ICC-approved common carrier rates. But these duties might reasonably be regarded as consistent with a more lenient attitude toward granting surface authority to air carriers through the normal surface certification process and with permitting a special higher trucking rate scale to accommodate the needs of air carriers. Such policies would, however, enhance the ability of the air carriers to compete with existing surface carriers. Therefore, it appears that protection of existing operators from competition is indeed the underlying motivation for these ICC-administered impediments to integrated, expedited freight service. On the other hand, the CAB's virtual exclusion of surface carriers from direct air carriage seems to have been at least in part the result of more than routine protectionism—that is, a desire to ensure that airline managements be singlemindedly devoted to the development of air transportation.[8]

**Price Regulation.** As part of the traditional apparatus of economic regulation imposed on the airline industry in 1938, full public utility–type controls governed the prices of the certificated route air carriers, including trunk, local, and all-cargo airlines, and covered both passenger fares and rates for the carriage of cargo. The commuter carriers, on the other hand, have been exempted as a class from price regulation, and the air freight forwarders were exempted from regulation of price level while remaining subject to the requirements that they file and adhere to tariffs and refrain from discrimination. As has been pointed out, ICC regulation of common carrier truck rates has also significantly affected the air freight industry.

### Effects of Economic Regulation

In spite of the imposing network of protectionist and jurisdictional controls surrounding the U.S. domestic air cargo industry, it has undergone an impressive expansion since its small beginnings in the 1940s. Combination carriers and all-cargo carriers have experienced a steady growth in traffic over most of the postwar period with the cooperation of a burgeoning group of air freight forwarders, and in recent years commuter carriers have met with outstanding success

---

[8] See L. S. Keyes, *Federal Control of Entry into Air Transportation* (Cambridge, Mass.: Harvard University Press, 1951), pp. 254–256.

in providing high-quality air freight service on a broad geographic scale.[9]

Nevertheless, some aspects of the industry's performance suggest that economic regulation may have had significant undesirable effects. A leading example is the serious deficiency of prime-time cargo airlift in important domestic markets in the mid-1970s, which suggests the possibility that overly restrictive route or rate control may have contributed to the shortage. Second, the conspicuously low load factors which have for many years been experienced in the bellies of combination aircraft raise the question whether regulatory restrictions on carrier pricing have prevented more intensive utilization of this capacity. Third, there is direct evidence that in some instances restrictions on the operating authority of cargo airlines have added unnecessarily to their costs. Finally, it appears that limits on operating authority such as those on the surface operations of the direct air carriers and the direct air transportation activities of forwarders and surface carriers may have been important obstacles to the development of fully integrated, high-quality freight transportation. The following section will review some readily available evidence bearing on the existence and significance of these suggested flaws in the prereform regulatory environment.

**Shortage of Freight Airlift: the Effect of Controlled Entry.** As shown in Tables 1 and 2, freighter air service by the combination carriers experienced spectacular growth during the latter part of the 1960s and provided an ever greater proportion of the total domestic all-cargo airlift in spite of the considerable expansion of the traffic of the all-cargo carriers. In 1970 combination carrier freighter traffic reached its peak of some 1,162 million revenue ton-miles, representing about 82 percent of the national total. By 1976 combination carrier freighter traffic had declined by close to 28 percent and ac-

[9] The largest of the commuter cargo carriers, Federal Express Corporation, began operations in April 1973; for the year ended May 31, 1976, it reported operating revenues of $75 million and net profit of $3.7 million. According to *Barron's* (March 13, 1978), Federal Express's revenues were running at an annual rate of $150 million in the spring of 1978. Taking advantage of the regulatory exemption available to users of small aircraft, this company built up a high-speed, reliable system of freight transport reaching seventy-eight airports (as of March 1978) and carrying parcels of up to a maximum weight of seventy pounds. The carrier's flexible, hub-and-spoke service pattern together with its efficient pick-up and delivery facilities is well adapted to providing expedited transportation to and from a large number of relatively small traffic sources to widely scattered destinations, despite the fact that traffic between any two points may be subject to often unpredictable daily fluctuations. A similar service has been developed by Summit Airlines, the second largest commuter cargo airline.

counted for only about 65 percent of the domestic total. The major part of this decline occurred in 1974 and 1975. Because of a marked expansion in the traffic of the all-cargo airlines, which occurred for the most part in 1972 and 1973, *total* freighter carriage in 1976 showed a decrease of less than 10 percent as compared with 1970, although it was down by about 21 percent from its peak in 1973.

These traffic figures do not fully reflect the decrease in freighter capacity offered by the combination carriers; freighter load factors (actual weight carried as a percentage of capacity weight) experienced by these airlines showed a marked increase from 1970 to 1973 (from 44.8 to 54.3 percent) and thereafter held steady (53.8 percent in 1974, 52.6 percent in 1975, and 53.6 percent in 1976). Measured by available ton-miles, trunkline freighter capacity in 1976 amounted to only about 60 percent of the level reached in 1970; for 1977 the corresponding figure was 62.5 percent. By contrast, available ton-miles

## TABLE 1

ANNUAL GROWTH RATES OF REVENUE TON-MILES IN DOMESTIC FREIGHTER SERVICE, COMBINATION AND ALL-CARGO CARRIERS, 1964–1977

| | *Percentage Change over Previous Year*[a] | | |
|---|---|---|---|
| Year | Combination carriers | All-cargo carriers | Total domestic operations |
| 1964 | 36.6 | 35.6 | 36.2 |
| 1965 | 46.4 | 12.8 | 33.4 |
| 1966 | 40.2 | 14.3 | 31.7 |
| 1967 | 41.0 | (4.8) | 28.0 |
| 1968 | 32.9 | 6.8 | 27.4 |
| 1969 | 13.6 | 8.2 | 12.6 |
| 1970 | 11.1 | 20.3 | 12.7 |
| 1971 | (5.9) | 6.6 | (3.6) |
| 1972 | 3.3 | 22.0 | 7.0 |
| 1973 | (0.4) | 47.6 | 10.6 |
| 1974 | (11.8) | (1.2) | (8.6) |
| 1975 | (11.3) | (11.7) | (11.4) |
| 1976 | (4.7) | 2.7 | (2.2) |
| 1977 (fiscal) | 0.7 | 3.9 | 1.7 |

[a] Figures in parentheses denote decreases in revenue ton-miles.

SOURCE: Civil Aeronautics Board, *Trends in Scheduled All-Cargo Service,* September 1977.

## TABLE 2

### Revenue Ton-Miles in Domestic Freighter Service, Combination and All-Cargo Carriers, 1963–1977

(thousands)

| Year | Combination Carriers | All-Cargo Carriers | Total Domestic Operations |
|------|---------------------|--------------------|---------------------------|
| 1963 | 175,223 | 111,854 | 287,077 |
| 1964 | 239,347 | 151,659 | 391,006 |
| 1965 | 350,356 | 171,097 | 521,453 |
| 1966 | 491,115 | 195,486 | 686,601 |
| 1967 | 692,416 | 186,115 | 878,531 |
| 1968 | 920,037 | 198,775 | 1,118,812 |
| 1969 | 1,045,121 | 215,123 | 1,260,244 |
| 1970 | 1,161,624 | 258,726 | 1,420,350 |
| 1971 | 1,092,926 | 275,704 | 1,368,630 |
| 1972 | 1,128,727 | 336,246 | 1,464,973 |
| 1973 | 1,124,347 | 496,416 | 1,620,763 |
| 1974 | 991,402 | 490,639 | 1,482,041 |
| 1975 | 879,219 | 433,438 | 1,312,657 |
| 1976 | 837,891 | 445,268 | 1,283,159 |
| 1977 (fiscal) | 859,293 | 455,229 | 1,314,522 |

Source: Civil Aeronautics Board, *Trends in Scheduled All-Cargo Service.*

offered by the all-cargo airlines in 1976 exceeded the 1970 level by 50 percent and in 1977 by almost 59 percent.[10]

Table 3 shows the very uneven incidence of the decline among individual carriers. Most notable is the complete cut-off of freighter service by Eastern and Delta, which left the central southern and southeastern parts of the country largely without scheduled all-cargo service in major markets. By contrast, Northwest more than doubled its volume of all-cargo carriage, and TWA, American, and United maintained all-cargo traffic in 1976 which amounted to approximately 88, 80, and 66 percent, respectively, of their 1970 levels. The decline in all-cargo departures between 1972 and 1974 and its concentration in particular markets is further indicated in Table 4. This reduction in service occurred at a time when overall air cargo traffic was well above its 1972 level; in 1973 and 1974 air cargo revenue ton-miles in domestic scheduled service by the certificated carriers were about

---

[10] Civil Aeronautics Board, *Trends in All-Cargo Service*, September 1977, and Form 242 reports.

## TABLE 3

### REVENUE TON-MILES IN DOMESTIC FREIGHTER SERVICE, BY CARRIER, 1970–1977

(thousands)

| Carrier[a] | 1970 | 1971 | 1972 | 1973 | 1974 | 1975 | 1976 | Fiscal 1977 |
|---|---|---|---|---|---|---|---|---|
| American | 351,114 | 296,294 | 315,112 | 293,264 | 281,789 | 259,973 | 279,445 | 308,438 |
| Braniff | 30,690 | 22,950 | 25,378 | 27,932 | 30,933 | 31,123 | 29,361 | 28,458 |
| Continental | 4,680 | 22,162 | 15,643 | 5,694 | 0 | 0 | 0 | 0 |
| Delta | 25,554 | 18,568 | 17,630 | 13,192 | 0 | 0 | 0 | 0 |
| Eastern | 69,699 | 92,232 | 113,745 | 109,511 | 43,685 | 39,867 | 0 | 0 |
| Northwest | 30,724 | 38,049 | 29,197 | 41,311 | 48,595 | 49,339 | 66,037 | 64,073 |
| Pan American | 46,628 | 46,634 | 29,879 | 29,640 | 25,879 | 19,191 | 26,686 | 30,184 |
| TWA | 181,024 | 149,788 | 161,216 | 164,746 | 172,139 | 155,980 | 159,630 | 157,103 |
| United | 420,318 | 405,799 | 420,927 | 439,057 | 388,382 | 323,796 | 276,732 | 270,936 |
| Airlift | 45,664 | 28,518 | 46,903 | 69,295 | 80,467 | 71,804 | 78,006 | 100,721 |
| Flying Tiger | 213,062 | 247,186 | 289,343 | 427,121 | 410,172 | 361,634 | 367,262 | 354,508 |

[a] National reported no freighter service during the period. Western provided a relatively small amount of freighter service in 1970 only.

SOURCE: Civil Aeronautics Board, Trends in Scheduled All-Cargo Service.

9

# TABLE 4

## FREIGHTER DEPARTURES AT MAJOR DOMESTIC AIRPORT CITIES, 1972 AND 1974

| City | 1972 | 1974 | 1974 as Percent of 1972 |
|---|---|---|---|
| Atlanta | 4,168 | 2,028 | 48.7 |
| Baltimore | 962 | 564 | 58.6 |
| Boston | 2,277 | 1,810 | 79.5 |
| Charlotte | 1,563 | 9 | —ᵃ |
| Chicago | 14,555 | 12,037 | 82.7 |
| Cleveland | 1,866 | 936 | 50.2 |
| Dallas | 3,110 | 2,553 | 82.1 |
| Denver | 1,250 | 486 | 38.9 |
| Detroit | 3,222 | 2,239 | 69.5 |
| Honolulu | 1,899 | 2,306 | 121.4 |
| Houston | 1,081 | 803 | 74.3 |
| Kansas City | 910 | 585 | 64.3 |
| Los Angeles | 8,872 | 8,511 | 95.9 |
| Miami | 1,678 | 569 | 33.9 |
| Minneapolis | 915 | 546 | 59.7 |
| New York | 9,873 | 7,946 | 80.5 |
| Newark | 3,482 | 1,521 | 43.7 |
| Philadelphia | 2,719 | 2,489 | 91.5 |
| St. Louis | 1,253 | 705 | 56.3 |
| San Francisco | 6,831 | 6,603 | 96.7 |
| Seattle | 1,893 | 1,826 | 96.5 |
| Total (average percent) | 74,379 | 57,072 | 76.7 |

ᵃ Less than 1 percent.

SOURCE: Adapted from table provided by Federal Express, derived from data in CAB's *Airport Activity Statistics*. U.S. Congress, House, Subcommittee on Aviation of the Committee on Public Works and Transportation, *Hearings on Reform of the Economic Regulation of Air Carriers*, 94th Congress, 2d Session, 1976, p. 93.

10 percent above the 1972 level. The sharpest reductions in service—to a number of departures less than 60 percent of the 1972 figure—occurred in nine cities: Atlanta, Baltimore, Charlotte, Cleveland, Denver, Miami, Minneapolis, Newark, and St. Louis. Departures from five of these cities (Atlanta, Charlotte, Denver, Miami, and Newark) were less than half of 1972 totals. Seven of the nine cities experiencing sharp reductions (the exceptions being Cleveland and Newark) were largely dependent on the combination airlines for air cargo

transportation. The impact of this concentrated reduction in service was severely felt by shippers and air freight forwarders alike.[11]

Service cutbacks in 1974 and 1975 were no doubt accelerated and deepened by the sudden rise in aircraft operating costs, which was largely due to the increased price of fuel.[12] However, this factor does not account for significant decreases in the other years of the 1970–1976 period, for the decline in freighter service by the combination airlines and the expansion of all-cargo airline carriage for the period as a whole, or for the geographic distribution of the reduction.

In view of the fact that the combination carriers throughout the period possessed ample authority to provide all-cargo service in the affected markets, it cannot be said that entry regulation produced the shortage in a direct manner. Nevertheless, controlled entry was probably a crucial causal factor. In the first place, this control provided the combination carriers with an opportunity to reduce service quality with the expectation that potential competitors offering to provide better service would be frustrated by inability to obtain the necessary permission to enter their markets. During the period under consideration, the Civil Aeronautics Board had adopted an exceptionally restrictive attitude toward authorizing new competition,[13] and large amounts of belly space on combination aircraft were available for the (mostly daylight) transportation of air cargo at very low cost to the carrier. Thus it was only to be expected that cost-conscious airline managements should seek to take advantage of the oppor-

---

[11] See, for example, the testimony of Louis P. Haffer, executive vice-president and counsel, Air Freight Forwarders Association, in U.S. Congress, House, Subcommittee on Aviation of the Committee on Public Works and Transportation, *Hearings on H.R. 14623*, 94th Congress, 2d Session, 1976, pp. 178–191. Haffer pointed out (p. 183) that in "1972 there were over 74,000 nighttime departures of freighters from the major domestic airport cities. In 1974, this had dropped to 57,000 departures." While the decline in freighter departures was offset, to some extent, by an increase in the average capacity of the freighter aircraft, this effect was of minor quantitative significance. In 1972, 40.7 percent of revenue ton-miles of cargo were carried in B-707-300 aircraft; 34.5 percent in DC8-63s; 13.8 percent in DC8-50Fs; and 10.4 percent in 727-100s; for 1974 the corresponding percentages were 39.8, 37.6, 13.5, and 4.6. In the latter year the B-747 accounted for 4.2 percent of revenue ton-miles. (These statistics include international as well as domestic traffic.) CAB, *Trends in All-Cargo Service*, September 1977.

[12] As compared with their 1973 levels, operating expenses per revenue ton-mile for the domestic freighter services of the combination carriers were about 11 percent higher in 1974 and about 29 percent higher in 1975. Operating revenue per revenue ton-mile in 1974 was 6.8 percent above the 1973 level; for 1975 there was a corresponding 22 percent increase.

[13] On this point, see U.S. Congress, Senate, Subcommittee on Administrative Practice and Procedure of the Committee on the Judiciary, *Civil Aeronautics Board Practices and Procedures*, 94th Congress, 1st Session, 1975.

tunity to reduce freighter service where the existing competitive situation would permit them to do so. As has been noted, actual service reductions were indeed concentrated in these markets. Moreover, the carriers' expectations (if such they were) that entry would be restricted were not disappointed: attempts by Flying Tiger to add Atlanta, Charlotte, Baltimore, and Miami (as well as Cincinnati, Houston, and Dallas/Fort Worth) to its domestic route system met with no success at the CAB.[14] Thus, even if the prospect of regulatory protection had no effect on the decisions of the incumbent carriers, the fact of restricted entry made possible the deterioration in the quality of service.

**Shortage of Freighter Airlift: the Effect of Rate Regulation.** Available statistics that indicate domestic freighter service has been generally unprofitable suggest that the CAB has been unduly restrictive in its control of the level of freight rates. If these rates were indeed held too low, it would be reasonable to conclude that at least some portion of the freighter capacity shortage was the result of rate regulation. Despite evidence that the CAB's delay in granting prompt price increases to reflect the abrupt rise in fuel costs made some such services unprofitable and thus brought about a reduction in their supply,[15] and although the 10 percent rise in general commodity rates in 1978 may indicate that the rates had failed to keep pace with the inflation in costs,[16] rate regulation does not appear to have been an influential factor in the recent sharp deterioration in freighter service in certain domestic markets.

If the statistical evidence (as shown in Table 5) is taken at face value, the conclusion is inescapable that profits in domestic scheduled freighter carriage have been elusive indeed. From 1963 through 1976, there appears to have been only one year, 1966, in which operating revenues exceeded operating expenses for the industry as a whole or for the combination airlines taken by themselves. The all-cargo carriers achieved a positive result in only two years—1966 and 1973.

---

[14] *AirCargo Magazine*, June 1977.

[15] In Table 5, note the sharp increase in the operating ratios for 1974 and 1975 as compared with 1973. Commenting on the failure of rates to reflect cost increases in this period, a cargo airline official attributed this development to "regulatory lag" rather than to deliberate policy. U.S. Congress, House, Subcommittee on Investigations and Review and Subcommittee on Aviation of the Committee on Public Works and Transportation, *Aviation Economics*, 94th Congress, 2d Session, 1976, pp. 463–464. Until 1973, the average cost of freighter service had trended generally downward; therefore significant losses resulting from "lag" could not have occurred in this period.

[16] Kahn, "Air Freight Forwarding," p. 8.

# TABLE 5

## Operating Ratios of Scheduled Domestic Operations of Combination and All-Cargo Carriers, 1963–1977

### (percent)

| Year | Combination Carriers | All-Cargo Carriers | Total Domestic Operations |
|------|--------------------|------------------|-------------------------|
| 1963 | 154 | 139 | 149 |
| 1964 | 131 | 127 | 130 |
| 1965 | 107 | 113 | 108 |
| 1966 | 98 | 93 | 97 |
| 1967 | 101 | 113 | 103 |
| 1968 | 101 | 132 | 106 |
| 1969 | 108 | 135 | 112 |
| 1970 | 117 | 116 | 117 |
| 1971 | 114 | 111 | 114 |
| 1972 | 111 | 101 | 109 |
| 1973 | 104 | 95 | 102 |
| 1974 | 109 | 116 | 111 |
| 1975 | 110 | 114 | 111 |
| 1976 | 100 | 101 | 100 |
| 1977 (fiscal) | 98 | 101 | 99 |

Note: Operating ratios are operating expenses divided by operating revenues.
Source: Civil Aeronautics Board, *Trends in Scheduled All-Cargo Service.*

If this evidence is considered in conjunction with Table 1, however, it becomes obvious that these operating losses did not prevent the general growth of the industry to its 1973 peak. This growth suggests that the loss statistics do not provide a fully accurate picture of actual operating results. Without attempting to engage in an exhaustive analysis of their origins, it may be noted that the cost allocation techniques which underlie these figures are "left to the discretion of the carriers"[17] and that revenues may in some instances be distorted by not taking into account important contributions to profitable connecting international operations (such as those of Flying Tiger).

It should be emphasized, however, that those losses which have been incurred cannot for the most part be attributed to CAB rate regulation. There is no evidence that the board has attempted to hold rates below the level of the carriers' actual costs; as the agency

[17] Civil Aeronautics Board, *Trends in All-Cargo Service*, September 1977, p. iii.

has remarked, its consistent policy has been to permit such rate increases as do not exceed industry average costs, and the carriers have been given "wide latitude in the pricing of their services."[18] Some close students of the field believe that profitable domestic freighter service became technically possible with the advent of jet freighters in 1963,[19] and at least one such student has attributed subsequent freighter unprofitability to "underpricing and overcompetition." However, this expert has not found an explanation for underpricing in regulatory policy. In fact, he has attributed freighter losses to mistaken decisions on the part of the carriers themselves.[20]

**Empty Belly Capacity: the Role of Minimum Rate Regulation.** Space available for cargo carriage in the bellies of combination aircraft has for many years been underutilized in terms of physical capacity. In 1974 a CAB expert witness testified that the load factor for this type of cargo capability was running in the neighborhood of 25 percent;[21] for 1975 Leister and Stram estimated the load factor between 26.4 and 29.4 percent.[22] This underutilization of combination aircraft cargo

[18] Civil Aeronautics Board, *Domestic Air Freight Rate Investigation*, Order 77-8-62 (1977), p. 6.

[19] See, for example, William E. O'Connor, *An Introduction to Airline Economics* (New York: Praeger, 1978), p. 103; and Lewis M. Schneider, *The Future of the U.S. Domestic Air Freight Industry* (Cambridge, Mass.: Division of Research, Graduate School of Business Administration, Harvard University, 1973), p. 3.

[20] Schneider, *Future of U.S. Domestic Air Freight*, p. 143: "The industry felt that prices had to be kept as low as possible without considering whether it wanted to stimulate emergency, routine perishable, or routine surface-divertible traffic. . . . The domestic freighter carriers during the 1965–1969 period were divided into two camps, the optimists and the conservatives. The optimists (American and United) poured on the capacity with little or no return. The conservatives (Trans World and Flying Tiger) lagged behind in additions to capacity, but usually suffered deficits, albeit on less investment. . . . The excessive competition and low load factors may have stemmed from the hope that increased capacity shares would produce disproportionately high market shares and profits. In fact, market shares were proportionate to capacity, and profits were not correlated well with capacity shares."

[21] Civil Aeronautics Board, *Domestic Air Freight Rate Investigation*, Docket 22859, Initial Decision of Administrative Law Judge (1975), p. 41.

[22] Leister and Stram, "Vertical Integration," pp. 244–248. The cited load factor figures are computed as a ratio between the weight of the traffic carried and the weight-carrying capacity of the part of the aircraft devoted to this type of traffic. Computed in terms of space occupied as compared with space available, load factors are somewhat higher but still quite low. A Flying Tiger official has recently testified that the average cargo density his airline had experienced with the DC-8 aircraft was in a ratio of 8.55/10 to the design density of the plane. House, Subcommittee on Investigations and Review and Subcommittee on Aviation of the Committee on Public Works and Transportation, *Aviation Economics*, p. 470. In this situation, the space load factor would amount to 117 percent of the weight load factor.

capacity suggests the possibility of overly restrictive minimum freight rate regulation—that is, of minimum rates which have been based on the full capacity costs of carriage in all-cargo aircraft rather than on the added costs of carriage in combination aircraft.

In the very early years of air freight carriage, minimum freight rates were in fact set on the indicated cost base and were continued in force for some years. This policy, adopted by the CAB in its first foray into the regulation of air freight rates, was intended to rescue the fledgling all-cargo air carriers from the threat to their survival posed by low freight rates proposed by the combination carriers.[23] This policy was gradually relaxed in subsequent years, and in 1961 the prescribed minimum was abandoned as no longer necessary. Thereafter, no comprehensive investigation of the air freight level and structure was undertaken until the early 1970s, and, as has been noted, the CAB's rate policy in the interim allowed the carriers a wide range of choice. In 1977 the board refused to adopt a restrictive minimum rate policy previously recommended by its administrative law judge; the policies that it did adopt were, moreover, shortly rendered moot by the enactment of P.L. 95-163.[24]

Thus, direct evidence indicates that rational pricing of belly freight transportation has not been hindered by regulatory policy. Nor is it necessary to invoke regulatory restriction to explain the phenomenon of underutilization; in fact, this cargo-carrying capacity has been largely determined by the demand for passenger service, and the unrestricted process of profit maximization would only coincidentally result in "full" utilization.[25] It is, of course, true that the profit-maximizing level of belly freight rates depends on the elasticity of the demand and hence on the availability of substitute sources of transportation, so that entry restraints may well have been partially responsible for underutilization in some markets.

**Cost Increases Induced by Regulation.** If operators of small aircraft had not been exempt from the certification requirement, such carriers as Federal Express and Summit probably would have been unable to develop their networks of expedited freight service or at the very least would have been delayed for long periods of time by the certification process. The usual certificate apparatus of fixed routings,

---

[23] Civil Aeronautics Board, Order 77-8-62, p. 5.

[24] See Chapter 2.

[25] This is not to deny that variation in the proportion of aircraft capacity devoted to passengers and cargo, respectively, is, at least to some extent, technically possible. See James C. Miller III, "The Optimal Pricing of Freight in Combination Aircraft," *Journal of Transport Economics and Policy*, vol. 7, no. 1 (1973).

restrictions for the protection of incumbents, and endlessly contested proceedings for the authorization of new service would have presented a dismaying prospect for any potential applicant,[26] and the CAB's extremely restrictive entry policy in the early 1970s would have further discouraged any hope of success. Under the circumstances, even an optimistic entrepreneur probably would not have been tempted to pursue a long and costly campaign for certification. But, in fact, the exemption did exist; like the early air-coach and all-cargo carriers, these innovative companies were able to wedge their way into the industry by means of a general exemption created with other kinds of operations in mind.[27] That these innovations were in fact possible is not due to any inherent virtue of the regulatory framework; they came into being not because of but in spite of the existence of regulation.

Nevertheless, it appears undeniable that the limits prescribed in the general exemption itself, together with an entirely reasonable refusal by the CAB to permit large-scale special exceptions merely to accommodate particular applicants, resulted in unnecessarily high-cost operations for a significant period and would have continued to do so if P.L. 95-163 had not been enacted. In 1975 Federal Express found that the volume of its traffic in some markets had outpaced the capacity which could be most economically provided by the small aircraft fitting within the ceiling in the commuter exemption; by its own estimate, inability to substitute larger aircraft on these routes was in 1976 adding to its daily costs by $30,000 to $40,000[28] and causing it to consume unnecessarily large amounts of aviation fuel.[29] An application by this carrier for authority to add five larger aircraft to its fleet was denied by the CAB on the ground that the proposal was "not appropriate for grant under the exemption provisions of section 416 of Act."[30] The basis for this decision was the unwillingness of the CAB to permit use of the exemption process to circumvent

---

[26] On the unsuitability of the certification apparatus for the operations of Federal Express and the prospects for expense and delay inherent in the process, see the testimony of Frederick E. Smith, in U.S. Congress, Senate, Subcommittee on Aviation of the Committee on Commerce, *Hearings on Regulatory Reform in Air Transportation*, 94th Congress, 2d Session, 1976, pp. 554–555.

[27] Keyes, *Federal Control of Entry*, chap. 5.

[28] U.S. Congress, House, Subcommittee on Aviation of the Committee on Public Works and Transportation, *Hearings on Reform of the Economic Regulation of Air Carriers*, 94th Congress, 2d Session, 1976, p. 953.

[29] House, Subcommittee on Investigations and Review and Subcommittee on Aviation of the Committee on Public Works and Transportation, *Aviation Economics*, p. 396.

[30] Civil Aeronautics Board, Order 75-12-38 (1975).

the protective purpose of certification;[31] in taking this stand, the agency was conforming to a fully justified interpretation of the law consistently supported by precedent. The attempts of Summit to obtain large aircraft authority were similarly frustrated by administrative action.[32]

The recent history of air freight provides other examples of obvious economic wastes resulting from protective regulation. Flying Tiger, which had a refueling stop and regular flights to Anchorage for many years on the way between the lower forty-eight states and the Orient, was repeatedly refused permission to carry freight between the contiguous United States and Anchorage in spite of the general availability of a large amount of empty carrying capacity on this route.[33] In the fall of 1976 a strike by the employees of UPS resulted in a flood of emergency traffic for Federal Express, which was physically unable to accommodate this traffic but applied for an emergency exemption to allow it to tender the excess to other airlines. Such an exemption would have provided a valuable service to shippers in need of a fast substitute for the suddenly unavailable UPS. After a delay of twelve and a half weeks, the CAB denied the application, three days after the end of the strike.[34] Taken by themselves, these examples are doubtless trivial in their quantitative impact. They are nevertheless indicative of the wasteful potential of regulation aimed at protecting particular markets.

In addition, some improvements in service and cost reductions would very likely have resulted from the entry of Seaboard and Pan American into important domestic markets (directly connected with their international routes) from which these carriers were excluded by the CAB.[35] Like most of the benefits of new competition, however,

---

[31] Ibid., p. 2, note 4: "In granting large-aircraft exemptions to air taxi operators, the Board has been careful to insure that such exempted operations would not be likely to have a significant impact on certificated carriers in the market. Indeed, the Board has often refused to grant exemptions in markets served by certificated carriers even though the proposed operations were much more limited than those envisioned here. . . . Thus, aside from the statutory limitations of the Board's exemption powers, we would not be prepared to conclude on the basis of contested pleadings that Federal Express's operations would not have a significant impact on certificated carriers and air freight forwarders."

[32] *AirCargo Magazine*, June 1977 and September 1977.

[33] Senate, Subcommittee on Aviation of the Committee on Commerce, Science, and Transportation, *Hearings on H.R. 14623*, p. 114.

[34] Senate, Subcommittee on Aviation of the Committee on Commerce, Science, and Transportation, *Regulatory Reform*, 1977, p. 484.

[35] Pan American had long been excluded from domestic markets as a matter of general CAB policy. Seaboard was not allowed to carry cargo from domestic points to its New York center of operations; largely because of this restriction, it had abandoned the domestic carriage of cargo. *Aviation Week*, January 23, 1978.

these probable effects cannot be quantitatively evaluated in the absence of actual experience. In these two cases, the postreform experience indicates that their importance might have been considerable (see Chapter 3).

**Regulatory Obstacles to Integration.** As has been suggested in the first section of this chapter, regulatory limitations on the extent of the PUD zone (and, before the reform legislation was passed, on the rates charged for surface transportation beyond its geographical limits) have provided a barrier to the extension of expedited freight service by the direct air carriers, and limitations on the substitution of surface for air carriage have had a similar result. While evaluation of the practical impact of these restrictions may not be possible, the leading all-cargo carrier, Flying Tiger, has taken the position that their removal is necessary for the provision of much-needed expedited freight transportation in markets where such services are now available,[36] and there seems to be no good reason for forcibly depriving this company of an opportunity to expand its service. Some students of the field have argued that maximum efficiency in air freight carriage always requires that the whole transportation function—from shipper to ultimate receiver—be performed by a single company.[37] Past experience provides no conclusive evidence on the general validity of this view, however. The integrated service offered by Federal Express has been successful, but it is not necessarily typical of the general air freight market. Federal Express is a relatively small overall operation, its air transportation activities are on a far smaller scale than those of Flying Tiger and the combination carriers, and the shipper clienteles served by the latter are more numerous and diversified. In any case, regulatory obstacles to one-company service appear to have no real economic justification.

Economic regulation of surface carriage, including control over operating authority geared to protecting the markets of existing surface operators, is primarily the responsibility of the ICC, although the CAB has concurred in these limitations. Therefore it appears that expanded opportunities for direct air carriers in this field, whether attained by liberalizing the controls over arrangements between air and surface carriers or by permitting broader common ownership of such services, will depend either on ICC administrative initiative or

---

[36] Senate, Subcommittee on Aviation of the Committee on Commerce, Science, and Transportation, *Regulatory Reform*, 1977, pp. 503–504. For further evidence, see Chapter 3, below.

[37] For example, Leister and Stram, "Vertical Integration."

on change in the legislation governing surface transportation. In light of past history and the ICC's recent action regarding the PUD zone (see Chapter 3), the latter alternative seems by far the more promising. Legislative change would probably also be necessary to promote integrated, expedited freight service by allowing existing air freight forwarders to obtain more extensive surface forwarding authority. Integration by means of expanded surface carrier participation in direct air transportation, as noted, has been blocked by a long-standing CAB policy, and here again legislation represents the only practical means of correction. The relevance of P.L. 95-163 to this problem will be touched on in Chapter 3.

Existing evidence also does not provide the basis for a definite answer to the question whether the inability of air freight forwarders to engage in direct air carriage foreclosed actual possibilities for the development of an integrated air freight service. The position that the foreclosure was not real may be defended on two grounds: (1) none of the existing forwarders was actively campaigning for direct air carrier authority, and (2) in spite of a long-standing legal ability to charter on a regular basis, examples of such activities by forwarders have been very few. As the CAB has noted, the only lasting arrangement of this nature that was not motivated by a desperate shortage of suitable airlift (normally provided by the direct air carriers) is the WTC-Shulman-Airlift transcontinental service which began in 1970 and has continued on a five-day-a-week basis in the ensuing years.[38] Can this absence of chartering be attributed to its inherent disadvantages as a substitute for direct authority, or does it give evidence of a general reluctance of air freight forwarders to take further responsibility for the transport function?

The CAB has argued that chartering was not deterred by any misgivings as to the genuineness or durability of the authorization under which it was conducted.[39] But it has suggested that a dampening effect may have been exercised by the regulation requiring open-ended access to charter flights in which more than one forwarder participates,[40] by the general unavailability of one-way charters, and

---

[38] Civil Aeronautics Board, *Air Freight Forwarders' Charters Investigation*, pp. 10–11, 17.

[39] Ibid., pp. 12–13.

[40] Ibid., p. 1: "This 'open-ended' requirement for joint loading arrangements presents an operational problem, in the case of charters, which is not present when forwarders are using scheduled service. The addition of another forwarder to a joint load assembled for a scheduled flight can only result in creating a larger shipment, thus possibly benefiting all forwarders participating in the arrangement. In the case of an arrangement in which two or more forwarders are sharing in the

by the unwillingness of forwarders to assume the financial risk of chartering an aircraft.[41] On the face of it, it would seem that a sufficiently large-scale, well-financed forwarding company could have surmounted all these obstacles without undue difficulty, so that chartering could have offered a good substitute for entry into direct air transportation. The virtual absence of such entry by forwarders may then have been due to their specialized nature; that is, having originated and prospered in their relatively limited and specialized function and operating in competition with direct air carriers who were free to deal with shippers as well as to provide transportation, the forwarders simply chose to continue to operate in the field in which they had proven to be qualified. If this analysis is correct, then the unavailability of direct operating authority cannot have prevented any real possibility of integrated services by forwarders. On the other hand, there may have existed other, less obvious disadvantages to using charters regularly compared with engaging in direct air carriage.

It is also undeniable that those forwarders, actual or potential, who might have contemplated a more ambitious use of charter service could reasonably have been discouraged by the prospect of the reaction of the certified carriers and the CAB to this expansion. This factor could also explain the absence of forwarder campaigns to obtain direct operating authority. Again, experience provides no definite answer to the broader question whether the general regulatory environment has hampered the development of integrated services by forwarders. In this connection, it should be noted that as of March 1979 a number of leading air freight forwarders had filed applications with the CAB to become direct air carriers under the new, reformed regulatory regime.[42]

## Conclusions

The conclusions reached here about the effects of regulation are based on readily available evidence, and some or all of them may need to be qualified in light of additional research. However, they do seem to give solid support to the view that protective regulation, and more particularly protective control over operating authority, has made possible the provision of inferior air freight service to the public, has

---

capacity of a charter flight, however, an additional forwarder must necessarily take away a portion of the space being used by one or more of the existing members of the arrangement."

[41] Ibid., pp. 16–17.

[42] *AirCargo Magazine*, March 1979.

caused unnecessary increases in costs of transportation in this field, and has placed unjustified obstacles in the way of the full development of expedited intermodal freight transportation on a broad geographical scale. To this writer, one of the most impressive parts of the story is the part that "didn't happen": that is, the fact that entry control did not prevent either certificated all-cargo or commuter airlines from gaining a foothold in the field, in each case because of an unplanned "loophole" in the regulatory framework. With regard to rate regulation, the evidence certainly does not prove the absence of any potential for harmful economic effects. It does, however, indicate that some plausible criticisms of such effects are not in fact justified. Two aspects of rate regulation that appear to have had harmful effects are the failure of freight rates promptly to reflect sharp increases in the price of aviation fuel and the ICC requirement that air carriers charge common carrier trucking rates for all surface carriage except that within the PUD zone.

The discussion here has, of course, been entirely concerned with the period preceding the enactment of legislation to reform the economic regulation of air cargo transportation, which will be discussed in Chapter 2. Chapter 3 will take up the question of the extent to which this legislation has corrected preexisting regulatory defects.

# 2

# Regulatory Reform: Origins and Content of the Air Cargo Legislation

The proposal for reform of air cargo regulation which developed into the law passed in November 1977 originated as a part of a more comprehensive program that encompassed air passenger transport regulation as well. For almost all its gestation period, the cargo measure was embedded in a larger plan, and it achieved separate identity only about three weeks before its final enactment. Therefore, the history of cargo reform is closely intertwined with that of the passenger reform proposals. Here, however, the passenger-related programs will be touched on only to the extent necessary to put the cargo development in historical perspective and to contrast its progress with that of the passenger plan.

The first set of airline regulatory reform proposals—one sponsored by the Ford administration, a second by Senator Edward M. Kennedy, and a third by the Civil Aeronautics Board—was considered by congressional committees in the spring and summer of 1976. In the following congressional session two measures were introduced into the Senate—one a compromise between the earlier Kennedy and administration proposals and the other a somewhat altered version of the 1976 CAB bill—and in the late summer of 1977 a House bill appeared, whose chief sponsor was Representative Glenn M. Anderson. The following discussion deals with these measures as they relate to air cargo and with the reactions to them by the parties chiefly affected.

All the reform proposals (like similar proposals for the reform of surface transport regulation) have a common background in the work of scholars at universities and policy research institutions. For many years before the actual introduction of reform legislation, scholars had been advocating liberalization, with growing response in governmental circles. In the airline field, the framers of reform legislation both in the administration and in Congress drew on the work of professional economists, and the Civil Aeronautics Board justified its reform program largely on the basis of academic economic analysis.[1] As a leading cargo airline executive has remarked, "The push for deregulation started not in the business community, but in the universities. The movement spread from academia to the executive and legislative branches of the government and finally found acceptance among the public at large."[2]

With respect to the airlines, however, this scholarly work had been concerned almost exclusively with passenger transportation. Moreover, the first legislative proposals submitted by congressional and administration sources reflected no special consideration of the problems and possibilities of air cargo regulation. In fact, the first reform legislation to give special treatment to air cargo was submitted to Congress by the Civil Aeronautics Board.

## The First Group of Airline Regulatory Reform Proposals, 1975–1976

Of the three proposals for airline regulatory reform which were presented to the 94th Congress, only that of the CAB provided special treatment for the air cargo industry as distinguished from air transportation as a whole.[3] The one sponsored by Senator Kennedy would have brought about basic reform of the entire airline regulatory scheme, covering cargo as well as passenger transportation, after a four-year transition period during which price and entry controls were to be progressively loosened.[4] At the end of four years,

---

[1] See, for example, Paul W. MacAvoy and John W. Snow, eds., *Regulation of Passenger Fares and Competition among the Airlines*, Ford Administration Papers on Regulatory Reform (Washington, D.C.: American Enterprise Institute, 1977); Senate, Subcommittee on Administrative Practice and Procedure of the Committee on the Judiciary, *Civil Aeronautics Board Practices and Procedures*, especially section 2; the testimony in support of S. 2551 in Senate, Subcommittee on Aviation of the Committee on Commerce, Science and Transportation, *Regulatory Reform*, 1976; and the testimony of CAB Chairman John E. Robson at the same hearings (especially on p. 377).

[2] Wayne M. Hoffman, "Regulation of Transportation: How Much is Enough?" *Transport 2000 and Intermodal World*, May/June 1978, p. 22. He continued: "What is remarkable about all of this is that many of the businessmen most directly affected . . . by the proposed deregulation have been fighting it tooth and nail."

[3] U.S. Congress, Senate, S. 3536, 94th Congress, 2d Session, introduced June 8, 1976.

[4] U.S. Congress, Senate, S. 3364, 94th Congress, 2d Session, introduced May 3, 1976.

entry control aimed at protecting the revenues of individual carriers was to be abandoned and public utility-type price control virtually eliminated. The administration bill, although arguably as progressive as political realities would permit, provided for no such basic reform.[5] This proposed legislation, equally applicable to passenger and cargo carriers, would have established a five-year transition period, during which price and entry controls were to be cautiously liberalized, followed by a somewhat less guarded program of limited "automatic" entry.

The CAB's reform program for passenger transportation was even more cautious than that of the administration, and its prospective practical impact would have been almost entirely dependent upon administrative discretion. However, the CAB's cargo program was clearly defined and, in the best sense of the term, radical. As Chairman John E. Robson announced on April 8, 1976, the CAB recommended "open entry, exit, and pricing in the domestic air freight industry," with board jurisdiction over such transactions as mergers to be discretionary rather than mandatory.[6] In an accompanying statement and in the CAB's draft legislation introduced early in June,[7] it was made clear that (1) the reform was to apply to overseas as well as interstate operations; (2) protective entry control was to be replaced by a simple fitness test after a two-year period of transition;[8] (3) price regulation designed to prevent discrimination, preference or prejudice, and predation would be continued under the new law, as well as the requirement that cargo tariffs be filed and adhered to; and (4) companies already certificated to provide all-cargo air transportation would immediately be authorized to engage in interstate air cargo transportation without geographic limit (as well as overseas air transportation to the extent provided in the certificate).

---

[5] U.S. Congress, Senate, S. 2551, 94th Congress, 2d Session, introduced October 22, 1975.

[6] Senate, Subcommittee on Aviation of the Committee on Commerce, Science, and Transportation, *Regulatory Reform*, 1976, p. 359. The following discussion of legislative proposals will not devote specific attention to exit control. The proposals for ultimate open entry as well as for interim "grandfather" authority all involve an absence of geographic limitations (within broad areas) which implies open exit as well as open entry in any particular market.

[7] Senate, S. 3536, 1976.

[8] During this two-year period, the CAB was empowered to subject interstate or overseas air cargo operating authority to "such reasonable terms, conditions, and limitations on the geographic, operational, and other scope of air transportation to be performed as the public interest [should] require," but these conditions were to become ineffective at the end of the period.

These recommendations were in important respects identical to proposals put forward by the CAB's Special Staff on Regulatory Reform in a report made public in the summer of 1975.[9] This Staff's report advocated open entry into domestic air cargo transportation after a two-year transition period and strictly limited the scope of price regulation in this field.[10] The CAB also followed the Staff in presenting its cargo program as one of a group of three proposals (for air cargo, air commuter, and charter transportation) designed to effect speedy liberalization in certain limited zones. Both the CAB and the Special Staff made essentially the same case for the adoption of these reforms: that is, that the benefits of free competition could be promptly secured without any serious impact on the finances of the certificated carriers; and the specific benefits sought were described by both in practically identical terms. To quote the CAB's statement:

> Open entry into cargo transportation, coupled with elimination of freight rate regulation can be expected to (1) maintain or enhance the quality of all-cargo service, and possibly lead to lower rates than otherwise would be charged; (2) offer the potential for long-run improvements in carrier efficiency, rates, and service, as well as the expansion into new markets that are now served primarily by sur-

---

[9] Civil Aeronautics Board, *Report of the CAB Special Staff on Regulatory Reform*, July 1975. This Staff, set up "for the express purpose of independently and objectively studying the need for regulatory reform," was headed by Roy Pulsifer, assistant director of the CAB's Bureau of Operating Rights. Other members of the CAB's permanent staff who participated in the preparation of the report were economists Willard L. Demory and James A. McMahon, and economic statistician Paul Eldridge. The fifth member of the Special Staff was the present writer. The CAB itself did not supervise preparation of the report and had no knowledge of its content before it was made public. The Staff's cargo proposal, like the other two recommendations for liberalized zones, was originated by Pulsifer, who also formulated the supporting arguments.

[10] The major difference between the two sets of cargo recommendations was in their prescription for regulatory policy in the two-year period of transition. The board did not accept the Staff's proposal for a freeze on the all-cargo authority of existing carriers during the transition period, nor did it adopt the Staff's suggestion of immediate open entry into the carriage of high-density freight and into geographic markets not receiving a specified minimum level of service for a specified period of time. (The actual importance of the former proposal would have depended on how "density" was defined and measured; obviously, the Staff's intent was that the definition confine the sphere of decontrol to a very small portion of the existing traffic.) In addition, the board's own proposal for immediate nationwide operating rights for all-cargo certificate holders had no parallel in the Staff report.

face transport; and (3) result in limited adverse impact on existing combination or all-cargo carriers.[11]

The similarity between the cargo programs of the two groups is in marked contrast to their sharp disagreement with respect to air passenger transport regulation. In this field the Special Staff had recommended putting an end to protective entry control after a period of three to five years.

## Reaction to the First Group of Legislative Proposals

At the hearings on the first group of reform proposals,[12] suggested reforms related to passenger transportation were extensively discussed, notably by representatives of the combination carriers who presented the conventional arguments in opposition to basic change. Little attention was devoted to cargo transportation, with the outstanding exception of the testimony of Frederick W. Smith, chairman of the board of Federal Express Corporation.[13] Smith, whose attempt to obtain authority to use larger aircraft had recently been frustrated by the CAB (see Chapter 1), welcomed the prospect of regulatory reform. After outlining his company's pressing need for larger aircraft, the unsuitability of traditional certification for its operations, and the very high probability of a delay of from two to ten years before certification could be granted, he went on to declare that Chairman Robson's proposal to "deregulate the industry" would be "perfectly acceptable" to Federal Express. Alternatively, he suggested broadening the CAB's exemption powers as they applied to all-cargo operations or changing the route authorization procedure so that it could not be "used as a weapon" to prevent entry into air cargo transportation.[14]

---

[11] Senate, Subcommittee on Aviation of the Committee on Commerce, Science, and Transportation, *Regulatory Reform*, 1976, p. 388. The entire discussion of cargo reform in the statement entitled "Legislative Regulatory Reform Program of the Civil Aeronautics Board" is very largely made up of language to be found in the *Report of the Special Staff*, on pp. 322, 325, and 331–332. The same is true of the board's statement on S. 292, submitted in the spring of 1977, and reproduced in Senate, Subcommittee on Aviation of the Committee on Commerce, Science, and Transportation, *Regulatory Reform*, 1977, pp. 193–196; and the statement on H.R. 8813, submitted the following summer, and reproduced in U.S. Congress, House, Subcommittee on Aviation of the Committee on Public Works and Transportation, *Aviation Regulatory Reform*, 95th Congress, 1st Session, 1977, pp. 160–161.

[12] Senate, Subcommittee on Aviation of the Committee on Commerce, Science, and Transportation, *Regulatory Reform*, 1976.

[13] See Chapter 1, note 8.

[14] Senate Subcommittee on Aviation of the Committee on Commerce, Science, and Transportation, *Regulatory Reform*, 1976, p. 558.

Later in the same month (April 1976), Smith specified further the characteristics of a system of entry control which he believed to be appropriate for air cargo transportation. At hearings before the House Aviation Subcommittee and the Subcommittee on Investigation and Review, he recommended: (1) that all-cargo carriers be certificated without specified points or routes to be served, on either a nationwide or other area basis; (2) that the all-cargo air carriers' service obligation be limited to the physical capacity of the carriers' equipment; (3) that certification of all-cargo carriers be granted on the basis of a showing of fitness, willingness, and ability; and (4) that the cargo authority of the combination carriers be limited to their certificated route systems.[15]

After the CAB-sponsored legislation was introduced in June, Smith indicated his strong support for its entry and pricing provisions with respect to air cargo but pointed out that, since no "grandfather" authority was granted for the exempt carriers, Federal Express's immediate need for larger aircraft would not be satisfied.[16] As will be seen, in legislation introduced in the next Congress this defect was remedied.

The position taken by the leading certificated all-cargo carrier in the domestic market, the Flying Tiger Line, was at this point much less clear. On the day following Smith's first House testimony, Tiger's chairman of the board, Wayne M. Hoffman, submitted a statement indicating that although he preferred total, immediate deregulation of air cargo and related motor transportation to any of the reform proposals, an unregulated market would be "counter to the best interests of the shipping public"—apparently because he expected such a market to bring about excessively low rates and reductions in service. Hoffman also argued that significant cargo service improvements could and should be achieved without amending the Federal Aviation Act, provided that certain steps were taken by the CAB and the ICC. These steps, which were nicely tailored to solve the company's immediate problems, included: (1) certification of

---

[15] House, Subcommittee on Investigations and Review and Subcommittee on Aviation of the Committee on Public Works and Transportation, *Aviation Economics*, pp. 400–402. I know of no instance of a certificated carrier being penalized for not accepting traffic beyond the capacity of its equipment.

[16] U.S. Congress, House, Subcommittee on Aviation of the Committee on Public Works and Transportation, *Reform of the Economic Regulation of Air Carriers*, 94th Congress, 2d Session, 1976, p. 953. Also at these hearings, support for general liberalization of airline regulation was expressed by representatives of contract air carriers, one of whom was a specialist in the carriage of air cargo. See pp. 960–962.

all-cargo air service "where the Board finds that an improved service would be provided whether the applicant proposes initially to utilize aircraft or a properly authorized motor carrier service"; (2) reduction or elimination of overlapping CAB and ICC regulation which was impeding the development of expedited intermodal freight service; and (3) flexible price regulation, including abandonment of maximum (but not minimum) rate regulation if the proposed entry policy were adopted.[17]

In his oral testimony, Hoffman appeared to be far more hospitable to the idea of reform and emphasized the ability of his company to survive and thrive in a more competitive environment. The problem, he indicated, was the "transitional chaos" and disadvantage to an existing carrier—as compared with new entrants—if there were no protection for it during the transition to the "completely unregulated" market, because time would be needed for adapting its fleet to the requirements of the new service patterns.[18] A statement submitted later in response to a committee member's request expressed Flying Tiger's support for the creation of a nonregulated market, provided that the opening of air freight markets to its competitors was accompanied by an opening of passenger markets to Flying Tiger, and that during a "reasonable transition period" the suggested steps be taken to facilitate unified provision of air and surface transport and loosen maximum price regulation.[19]

In spite of these apparent indications of convergence between

---

[17] House, Subcommittee on Investigations and Review and Subcommittee on Aviation of Committee on Public Works and Transportation, *Aviation Economics*, pp. 457–458.

[18] Ibid., p. 474: "I am sitting here with $200 million worth of stretch DC-8's which may not fit a completely unregulated type of market. First of all, I would be permitted to serve cities that I am not now permitted to serve, so I would broaden my service area tremendously. I would require an entirely different set of aircraft to do that kind of job. I cannot get from where I am now with equipment that may under that type of environment be obsolete or obsolescent to where I want to be simply overnight. In that period of time, a vested carrier is going to take a beating. The new entrant is not going to take that beating. Is there any reason why I, who have been struggling since 1945, should be the one to suffer that kind of transitional pain? If you will protect us in that transition, we would be happy to get out and compete on a level-handed basis." However, Hoffman later expressed the view that, "Even assuming an abrupt transition to complete and sudden deregulation, the existing companies, efficiently run, with skilled managers in place, with plant and equipment currently operational, have an enormous advantage over new entrants." This quotation is from Hoffman, "Regulation of Transportation."

[19] House, Subcommittee on Investigations and Review and Subcommittee on Aviation of the Committee on Public Works and Transportation, *Aviation Economics*, pp. 477–478.

the positions of Federal Express and Flying Tiger, the former's efforts in 1976 to get agreement on basic reform proved unsuccessful.[20] The certificated all-cargo carriers also opposed the attempt of Federal Express later in the same year to obtain legislation broadening the CAB's exemption powers governing the operation of parties with pending applications for all-cargo certificates; this attempt also failed. At these hearings, a representative of the Air Freight Forwarders Association presented forceful testimony corroborating the evidence presented by Federal Express regarding the decline in freighter service and the consequent difficulties confronting the freight forwarder industry.[21] In contrast to most of the debate on air cargo reform, these hearings were marked by some amusing examples of the exaggerated rhetoric often used in the past by advocates of the status quo in transport regulation.[22]

## The Second Group of Reform Proposals, Winter-Spring 1977

Both the general airline regulatory reform bills introduced early in the next congressional session provided for open entry into the field of domestic and overseas air cargo transportation after approximately two years. The one sponsored by Senators Howard W. Cannon and Edward M. Kennedy embodied a compromise between the Kennedy and administration bills of the previous session.[23] Compared with the earlier Kennedy proposal, its provisions with respect to passenger service represented a substantial retreat. This proposed legislation

[20] See U.S. Congress, Senate, Subcommittee on Aviation of the Committee on Commerce, *Hearings on S. 3684*, 94th Congress, 2d Session, 1976, p. 14; and House, Subcommittee on Aviation of the Committee on Public Works and Transportation, *Hearings on H.R. 14623*, pp. 56–57.

[21] Testimony of Louis P. Haffer, executive vice-president and counsel, Air Freight Forwarders Association, in House, Subcommittee on Aviation of the Committee on Public Works and Transportation, *Hearings on H.R. 14623*, pp. 178–189.

[22] Testimony of Robert W. Prescott, president of Flying Tiger Line, Inc., in Senate, Subcommittee on Aviation of the Committee on Commerce, *Hearings on S. 3684*, p. 53, to the effect that in the absence of protective regulation, air transportation would be in a "jungle" and also in an "Ice Age." The record contains other examples: As late as April 1977 the president of Seaboard World Airlines, Richard M. Jackson, warned that, in supporting liberalized air transport regulation, the "politicians may be pulling us into the quicksands of democracy" (*AirCargo Magazine*, April 1977, p. 64). Shortly before the passage of the cargo reform legislation in the fall of that year, Representative Donald Fraser opposed the measure on the ground that he was unconvinced that "automatic entry and exit will not result in wholesale loss of air service and loss of employment to thousands of skilled career airline employees" (*Congressional Record*, 95th Congress, 1st Session, vol. 123, November 2, 1977, p. H12050).

[23] U.S. Congress, Senate, *S. 689*, 95th Congress, 1st Session, introduced February 10, 1977.

29

did not definitely require or ensure the basic reform of the regulatory framework: the "public convenience and necessity" criterion for entry regulation was to be retained for the indefinite future. Consequently, the regulators might reasonably infer that the basic protective aim of the existing statute would remain in force. Like all the other general reform bills, this proposed legislation contained a revised declaration of policy which could conceivably have been read as requiring the abandonment of protectionism; but here as elsewhere the legislative context undercuts this interpretation.[24] Compared with the earlier administration proposal, Cannon-Kennedy was marginally more liberal in its approach to passenger transportation; for example, the effective date of liberalized entry provisions was advanced and the scope of permitted rate flexibility was broadened.

The Cannon-Kennedy bill's cargo provision, however, was a major step in the direction of reform. From the effective date of the legislation to January 1, 1979, applications for certificates to engage in interstate or overseas all-cargo air transportation were to be granted to fit, willing, and able applicants unless the CAB should find the transportation applied for was not consistent with the public convenience and necessity. After January 1, 1979, the latter requirement was to be dropped. In contrast to this basic reform in the sphere of entry regulation, there was no provision for special liberalization of the control of air freight pricing.

The other new bill, introduced by Senator James B. Pearson, was much the same as the CAB-sponsored proposal of the previous session, except that automatic grandfather authority without geographic limitation as to route was to be given to commuter cargo airlines as well as to the certificated all-cargo carriers.[25] (Grandfather authority was to be granted to all commuter carriers which had engaged continuously in scheduled all-cargo carriage from January 1, 1976, up to the effective date of the statute.) There was no change in the recommendation concerning freight rate regulation.

### Reaction to the Second Group of Legislative Proposals

By the time that hearings on these bills were held in March 1977, representatives of the major commuter carriers and Flying Tiger had

---

[24] This point is developed with respect to the earlier administration proposal in L. S. Keyes, "A Comparison of Two Proposals for Regulatory Change," *Journal of Air Law and Commerce*, vol. 41 (1975), p. 727. The Cannon-Kennedy measure also contains special procompetitive admonitions addressed to the interpretation of "public convenience and necessity," but the same essential objection still applies.

[25] U.S. Congress, Senate, *S. 292*, 95th Congress, 1st Session, introduced January 18, 1977.

formed a united front favoring the enactment of basic reform of air cargo regulation.[26] Their agreed position on entry and pricing was in most respects identical to that of the CAB, but they suggested a change in geographic scope so that certain operations normally included under the term "overseas" would not be covered by the new law and recommended authority for air cargo carriers to provide expedited freight services (by contract with ICC-licensed truckers) at air freight rates.[27]

The combination carriers continued to focus their efforts almost exclusively on criticizing proposals for the reform of passenger transport regulation. Spokesmen for both the freight forwarders and the National Industrial Traffic League (NITL) stressed the need for retaining rate regulation to prevent discrimination and opposed open entry in the cargo field. The league, representing shippers by surface as well as by air, recited the consensus of its membership that there should be "liberalization" of air cargo entry control but not "complete removal of restrictions."[28] It was the view of the Air Freight Forwarders Association that all-cargo certificates should continue to be confined to specified routes, since areawide or nationwide service was the particular function of the forwarders, but that, if the broader authority were to be authorized, the forwarders should be given the right to obtain it for themselves.[29] A representative of shippers of live animals favored the retention of the CAB's full complement of powers over freight rates.[30]

The president of the National Air Carrier Association, representing the supplementals, devoted most of his testimony to the passenger proposals. With respect to cargo, he merely noted that the association saw "no valid reason why public convenience and necessity considerations should be excluded entirely in the certification of all-cargo carriers," in keeping with the association's opinion "that reform measures should be applied evenhandedly to all segments of

---

[26] Their position is summarized in a statement submitted by Joseph J. Healy, executive vice-president and chief operating officer of the Flying Tiger Line, Senate, Subcommittee on Aviation of the Committee on Commerce, Science, and Transportation, *Regulatory Reform*, 1977, pp. 499–505. Representatives of Federal Express and the second largest commuter carrier, Summit Airlines, also testified in favor of the proposal.

[27] "Services for other areas such as Guam, Samoa, and the Trust Territories normally included in the definitions of overseas air transportation are substantially dissimilar from those for Puerto Rico and should continue to be regarded for air freight purposes similarly to foreign air transportation." Ibid., pp. 501, 503.

[28] Ibid., p. 1234.

[29] Ibid., pp. 1107–1113.

[30] Ibid., pp. 1526–1532.

the air transportation industry."[31] This general reasoning was useful in support of the supplementals' opposition to immediate open entry into their own field—that of charter transportation; in the air cargo field, their statement on entry control appeared, like that of the NITL, to be abstract and perfunctory.

Broader operating authority for the commuter cargo airlines was opposed by the Teamsters, who had experienced great difficulties in their attempts to organize the employees of these carriers, in part because, unlike the employees of the trucking companies and freight forwarders, they were not covered by the National Labor Relations Act.[32]

### The House Bill, Summer 1977

The reform legislation introduced in the House by Representative Anderson in August 1977 was broadly similar to Cannon-Kennedy in its application to air passenger transportation.[33] With respect to cargo, the House bill, like both of its Senate predecessors, provided for open entry into all-cargo air transportation after a short transition period. The CAB-sponsored legislation was followed in regard to freight rate regulation and in granting broad geographic grandfather authority to the certificated all-cargo carriers and to certain exempt cargo carriers.

Two major innovations were the inclusion of combination and supplemental carriers among those entitled to grandfather rights in all-cargo carriage and the shortening of the transition period from two years to one. Although the cargo carriers' request for additional authority in the field of surface carriage was not granted, a new special declaration of policy recognized the particular problems and possibilities of air cargo transportation. This policy declaration was carried over verbatim into the final legislation and is quoted here in full:

> The Board, in the exercise and performance of its powers and duties under this Act with respect to all-cargo air service shall consider the following, among other things, as being in the public interest:

[31] Ibid., p. 358.

[32] Ibid., pp. 703–721.

[33] U.S. Congress, House, *H.R. 8813*, 95th Congress, 1st Session, introduced August 13, 1977.

(A) The encouragement and development of an *expedited* all-cargo air service system, provided by private enterprise, responsive to (i) the present and future needs of shippers, (ii) the commerce of the United States, and (iii) the national defense.

(B) The encouragement and development of an *integrated* transportation system relying upon competitive market forces to determine the extent, variety, quality, and price of such services.

(C) The provision of services without unjust discriminations, undue preferences or advantages, unfair or deceptive practices, or predatory pricing. [Emphasis supplied.]

In addition, the geographic scope of the reform was revised to include transportation to and from Puerto Rico and the Virgin Islands while excluding other overseas traffic; in one significant (but temporary) backward step, a new provision governing grandfather authority for commuter carriers would have excluded all but the largest from eligibility.

The effect of the two major policy innovations was to eliminate or reduce competitive disadvantages which would have afflicted certain carriers if the CAB's proposal had been adopted without change. Supplemental and combination carriers which were currently providing all-cargo service (and had been doing so for a prescribed period) would, under the new bill, receive grandfather authority at the same time as the all-cargo carriers, and prospective initiators of new all-cargo service, including the forwarders and the remaining combination carriers, would be able to begin service, without a showing of public convenience and necessity, after one year rather than two.

### Reaction to the House Bill and Passage of P.L. 95-163

Although very extensive hearings on the House bill were held, opposition to its cargo provisions was so muted that a committee member who had participated in the proceedings was given the impression that no objection to them had been heard.[34] There was no formal appearance by any representative of the Teamsters. Spokesmen for the NITL and the National Air Carrier Association expressed the same views as they had in the Senate hearings, but serious opposi-

[34] Statement of Representative John P. Hammerschmidt, *Congressional Record*, 95th Congress, 1st Session, vol. 123 (November 2, 1977), p. H12048.

tion to the entry provisions was directed mainly to the drastic limit which the new bill would have placed on grandfather eligibility for the commuter carriers.[35] With respect to pricing, NITL and Air Freight Forwarder representatives continued to insist upon the need for preventing discrimination and requiring filing of and adherence to tariffs.[36] As before, the association of live animal shippers stood alone in advocating retention of the CAB's full power over freight rates.[37]

Representatives of Flying Tiger and of the two leading all-cargo commuter carriers testified in favor of the bill, although the former still urged broader authority for the cargo airlines in the field of surface transportation, opposed grandfather rights for the combination carriers, and suggested that the grandfather period be three years rather than one.[38] Even the two certificated all-cargo carriers who did not appear in support of the measure did not actively oppose it, although there is good evidence that Airlift suggested a postponement of the effective date of the reform until the CAB should approve this airline's pending application for international authority,[39] and, as noted, Seaboard's president had earlier publicly expressed misgivings about liberalized regulation.[40] Both these carriers have in fact taken advantage of domestic route opportunities opened under the new regime; it may be conjectured, therefore, that the prospect of obtaining these opportunities may have persuaded them to adopt a more favorable attitude toward the proposed legislation.

In view of the strong case made for cargo reform and the minor nature of the objections, it became evident that this measure could and should be promptly enacted. To extricate the cargo proposal from the delays and difficulties which continued to beset the general airline reform bill, Senator Cannon proposed to the House subcommittee that the cargo provisions be separated out and grafted onto H.R. 6010, a bill then in conference, which was made up of mis-

---

[35] House, Subcommittee on Aviation of the Committee on Public Works and Transportation, *Aviation Regulatory Reform*, pp. 981–985, 1164. For an example of opposition, see the testimony of John C. Emery, Jr., president and chief executive officer, Emery Air Freight Corporation, ibid., pp. 1261–1265.

[36] Ibid., pp. 2154–2156, 981–985.

[37] Ibid., pp. 1316–1319.

[38] Ibid., pp. 727–729, 1260.

[39] Remarks of Representative Claude Pepper, *Congressional Record*, 95th Congress, 1st Session, vol. 123 (November 2, 1977), p. H12045.

[40] See note 22, above. According to Tiger's counsel, J. W. Rosenthal, the company had the proxies of Seaboard and Airlift in supporting legislation for regulatory reform. *CAB Docket 32318*, Transcript of Oral Argument, October 19, 1978, p. 61.

cellaneous and relatively noncontroversial aviation measures.[41] This move was made on October 20, 1977.[42]

The version of H.R. 6010 that emerged from conference, was adopted by both houses, and signed by the president on November 9 contained much less restrictive eligibility conditions for grandfather authority for the commuter carriers than had the House bill.[43] Moreover, the wording of the conference report removed any doubt that air freight rates were to continue to be regulated to prevent discrimination and predation and also made clear that publication of and adherence to tariffs was expected to be required. Referring to a provision conferring upon the CAB power to exempt the air cargo carriers from most sections of the Federal Aviation Act, the report stated:

> While this section is intended to give the Board substantial discretion, the Managers do not contemplate that the Board will exempt carriers from the requirement of filing tariffs. Tariffs provide valuable notice of rates to users of air transportation. Tariffs will be necessary for the Board to effectively carry out its duties to determine whether rates for the transportation of property are discriminatory, preferential, prejudicial, or predatory.[44]

[41] Statement of Representative Hammerschmidt, *Congressional Record*, 95th Congress, 1st Session, vol. 123 (November 2, 1977), p. H12048. These measures included: (1) extension of the aviation war risk insurance program for five years, with expanded authority for the secretary of transportation to provide insurance risks other than war risks; (2) authorization of reduced-rate transportation for the elderly and handicapped on a space-available basis; (3) provision for payment of airline subsidies (to Ozark and Texas International) which had been withheld by the CAB; (4) authorization of aircraft registration by aliens and foreign corporations in the United States; (5) permission for small aircraft to operate temporarily without emergency locator transmitters when these were under repair or being serviced; (6) authorization for nonrepayment by Air Midwest of a subsidy received under a program later struck down by a court; and (7) extension of the advance filing requirements governing proposed tariff changes by direct and indirect air carriers, accompanied by a provision for CAB approval or disapproval of such proposed changes at least fifteen days before the effective date.

[42] *Congressional Record*, 95th Congress, 1st Session, vol. 123 (October 20, 1977), p. S17530.

[43] Signing of P.L. 95-163 reported in the *Washington Post* (November 10, 1977). The requirement that eligibility be contingent upon carriage of more than 20 million interstate revenue ton-miles of freight during the twelve-month period ending on the date of enactment was deleted. The law, however, contained a requirement that all-cargo air service in the grandfather period must have been scheduled and continuous and thus excluded the supplemental (charter) carriers.

[44] U.S. Congress, House, Conference Report to accompany H.R. 6010, House of Representatives Report no. 95-773 (October 27, 1977), pp. 14–15.

Thus two controversial features of H.R. 8813 were effectively removed from the final legislation. No answer was given to the remaining criticisms of Flying Tiger as to surface rights, the length of the transition period, and eligibility for grandfather authority, nor was any attempt made to provide full rate control as requested by one group of shippers.

In almost all other important respects, the final legislation followed H.R. 8813. There were, however, two additional changes: transportation within the states of Hawaii and Alaska was explicitly excluded from its scope,[45] and inadvertently, the supplemental carriers were made ineligible for grandfather authority. A remedy for this legislative lapse was immediately set in motion and became effective in March 1978 by the enactment of P.L. 95-245.[46]

During the congressional debate immediately preceding the enactment of P.L. 95-163, its chief sponsors, Representative Anderson and Senator Cannon, made statements that highlighted the most persuasive arguments for reform. For the most part, these arguments are concerned with the undesirable effect of existing regulation on the cost and quality of air cargo transportation service (and, by implication, the improvements in cost and service to be expected from reform). To quote Representative Anderson:

> The existing regulatory system governing domestic all-cargo service has not produced desirable results for the industry or for the shipping public. With few exceptions domestic all-cargo service has been unprofitable since 1967. Between 1965 and 1976 freighter operators accumulated $210 million in pretax losses.
>
> In the past few years, all-cargo service has been reduced substantially and cargo has moved on combination aircraft. The schedules of combination aircraft are geared to the needs of passengers who generally want to travel during daylight hours. By contrast shippers of cargo frequently de-

---

[45] This exclusion resulted from a limiting amendment offered in conference by senators from Hawaii and Alaska. *Congressional Record*, 95th Congress, 1st Session, vol. 123 (October 28, 1977), p. S18029.

[46] Commenting on this omission, Representative Anderson remarked: "This was an oversight as Senator Cannon indicated during the Conference. We recognized that this would work to the disadvantage of the supplemental air carriers who have been pioneers in all-cargo transportation and who possess the most modern freighter aircraft, but it was agreed to retain the language as proposed because of parliamentary considerations. In order to rectify this problem, I introduced yesterday H.R. 9851 with members Johnson, Snyder, and Hammerschmidt as cosponsors and I trust that this body will take prompt action on that bill." *Congressional Record*, 95th Congress, 1st Session, vol. 123 (November 2, 1977), p. H12045.

sire overnight service with late evening departures and early morning arrivals.

The failure of regulated service to meet the needs of shippers has been demonstrated by the recent growth in unregulated operations. A commuter carrier, Federal Express, began operating in 1973 and has quickly grown to a $100 million a year operation. A leading air freight forwarder, Emery Air Freight Service, has found scheduled air freight service to be deficient and has contracted for charter service in major markets.

The existing regulatory system prevents air carriers from adjusting their service and fares promptly to meet the demands of the marketplace. Under existing law, Federal Express, an all-cargo commuter, has been unable to get permission to substitute large aircraft for the multiple daily flights of small aircraft it now operates between a number of cities. The substitution of large aircraft would produce lower costs for Federal Express and significant reductions in the energy it uses.[47]

Senator Cannon called attention to the inefficient use of fuel and aircraft resulting from regulatory restrictions on routes and equipment and pointed out that the existing regulatory scheme was not necessary to maintain satisfactory standards of safety, to prohibit excessive prices, or to prevent over- or undersupply of air service in any individual market.[48]

Further light on the reasons for the prompt enactment of the cargo reform legislation was provided soon after its passage by David Heymsfeld, who served as assistant counsel in aviation for the House Committee on Public Works and Transportation during the period when the measure was under review. Explaining the history of the legislation at a forum sponsored by the Ad Hoc Committee on Airline Regulatory Reform (a group composed of representatives of various nongovernmental proreform organizations), Heymsfeld attributed the bill's passage to the existence of a "crying need to improve domestic all-cargo service" and to the fact that "Federal Express and Flying Tiger did an outstanding job in presenting their case to Congress." He also referred to the limited nature of the opposition and pointed

---

[47] Statement of Representative Anderson, *Congressional Record*, 95th Congress, 1st Session, vol. 123 (November 2, 1977), p. H12044.

[48] Statement of Senator Cannon, *Congressional Record*, 95th Congress, 1st Session, vol. 123 (October 20, 1977), pp. S17533–17534. The statement also contains an unexplained reference to an "artificial pricing structure that does not and cannot meet existing economic realities" and that involves "artificially high prices" for air cargo service users.

out that it was much weaker than the opposition to reform in air passenger transportation.[49]

## Summary and Conclusions

The major reforms embodied in the new law—open entry after a brief period, limited price control, and immediate expanded authority for some of the existing participants—were those which had been recommended by the CAB in its original proposal. Important changes made during the legislative process were both in a liberalizing direction: the transition period was cut in half, and the scope of the grandfather provision was considerably broadened. The attempts of certificated and commuter cargo carriers to narrow the scope of grandfather authority and increase the length of the grandfather period were unsuccessful, as was the forwarders' effort to confine all-cargo certification to specified routes. By contrast, the proposal for reform on the passenger side was bogged down in seemingly hopeless controversy; and, as has been noted, the one bill which had embodied genuine basic reform had failed early in the process as its sponsors adopted instead a gradualistic measure with a highly uncertain ultimate outcome.

Only about nineteen months elapsed between Chairman Robson's endorsement of basic reform of air cargo regulation before the Senate Aviation Subcommittee in April 1976 and the signing in November 1977 of P.L. 95-163, a law which abolished a scheme of regulation in existence for thirty-nine years. What factors were responsible for this truly remarkable development?

It is axiomatic that a complete list of the causal factors behind any event cannot be devised, since a multitude of conditions must exist to make its occurrence possible. Thus, if the nation's economy had been depressed, carrier finances more vulnerable, and the political climate of opinion more inclined toward governmental protectionism, air cargo reform might well have been ruled out. However, it seems useful to identify several particular factors which were essential for the passage of this reform.

First, the CAB had sponsored the proposal and forcefully defended it on the ground that air cargo was a field in which basic reform could be promptly achieved with little transitional disruption and with the assurance of important public benefits. Also important in bringing about the ultimate success of the cargo legislation was the prompt acceptance and support that administrative and congres-

---

[49] *Aviation Week*, December 19, 1977.

sional advocates of general airline regulatory reform had given to the idea of open entry into the cargo field after a brief transition period. Next should be cited the response of leading members of the air cargo transportation industry, who were ready to accept a far more radical change in the regulatory environment than would have been needed to solve their current problems—a change which involved a future for them without regulatory protection. It was the testimony of these representatives—mainly of Flying Tiger and Federal Express—which brought home to the concerned congressional committees the deficiencies in freighter service and unnecessary excess costs produced by the existing regulatory scheme. This testimony was therefore crucially influential in gaining congressional support. Finally, there was effective congressional sponsorship, provided by members who were openminded enough to appreciate the merits of this sharp departure from long-standing regulatory practice and to become actively instrumental in its adoption.

All these factors appear to have been necessary for the timely achievement of the reform. Without the enthusiastic support of the industry spokesmen, the measure would no doubt have been subject to the delays, difficulties, and dilutions besetting the passenger transport reform proposals advanced by the CAB and others. If there had been no CAB recommendation, industry initiatives would doubtless have continued to be confined, as they had been in the past, to campaigning for administrative relief for particular problems. Despite its long history of frustration at the hands of the CAB—notably in matters of route authority—Flying Tiger had sponsored no broad legislative reform, and Federal Express's response to regulatory restraint on choice of equipment had been, first, a request for special exemption by administrative means and, second, a proposal for a very limited legislative change. Without the CAB's action, pursuit of such limited initiatives would certainly have continued to seem more likely to succeed than a try for major legislative change. Finally, both government and industry efforts would evidently have been ineffective in the absence of active congressional sponsorship.

# 3

# Postreform Developments and Indications for the Future

It is of course too early to attempt a definitive assessment of the results of the enactment of the air cargo reform legislation. Expansion and improvement of the supply of air cargo transportation in its many and varied markets, the development of new price structures and price-service options, and the tempering of these initiatives by competitive response necessarily take time to materialize, especially since the resources and energies of the combination carriers during 1978 were to a great extent absorbed by the boom in passenger traffic which accompanied the CAB's de facto deregulation of the fare structure. This boom also resulted in a shortage of aircraft that has hampered the expansion of cargo service. The postreform economic regulatory framework has yet to be definitely established, and those not entitled to grandfather authority became eligible for open entry only on November 9, 1978. Yet, a review of some major postreform developments does provide a basis for a tentative evaluation of the effects of the new law as well as some indication of what may be expected for the future.

## Expansion of Freight Traffic and Service

Domestic air freight traffic carried by the all-cargo airlines showed a dramatic increase in 1978, when revenue ton-miles reached a level 26 percent higher than in 1977.[1] This increase may be compared with

---

[1] Testimony of Marvin S. Cohen, chairman, on behalf of the Civil Aeronautics Board, before the Senate Committee on Commerce, Science, and Transportation, April 5, 1979, p. 5. The corresponding percentage for Flying Tiger alone is over 33 percent, according to this testimony. It is here noted that the growth rates are "adjusted to factor out certain international shipments that were included as domestic shipments in 1978 and were included in the CAB's 'Air Carrier Traffic Statistics.' "

a 1969-1977 average annual growth rate of about 10 percent[2] and a 1976-1977 increase of 11 percent.[3] Trunkline freight traffic, on the other hand, increased by only 1.1 percent in 1978, as compared with a 7 percent growth in 1977[4] and a 1969–1977 average annual growth rate of 5 percent.[5] Because of this relatively poor trunkline performance, which the CAB has tentatively attributed to these carriers' "concentration on expanding and developing their passenger traffic during the same period,"[6] the level of traffic probably has not yet fully reflected the impact of deregulation. A major improvement in air freight service has already resulted from regulatory reform, however, with a marked increase in the availability of transportation in freighter aircraft. Freighter capacity operated by trunklines and all-cargo carriers in domestic service was 21 percent higher in calendar year 1978 than in 1977 (as compared with an increase of 4.5 percent in 1977 and a decrease of 7.7 percent in 1976).[7]

The expansion in freight capacity and volume obviously reflects in part the extension of Flying Tiger's operations into new geographical markets after its qualification for nationwide authority under the new law early in January 1978. According to a spokesman for this carrier, by the fall of 1978 it had added eight domestic terminals to the ten already served before the new law came into effect;[8] these include Anchorage, Atlanta, Dallas/Fort Worth, Houston, Charlotte, and Cincinnati, among which are important traffic centers that had suffered from the recent decline in service by all-cargo aircraft operated by the combination carriers.[9] In addition, the new pricing freedom has permitted Tiger to provide expedited service to at least twenty-one new cities by connecting surface trans-

---

[2] Leister and Stram, "Vertical Integration."

[3] Testimony of Marvin S. Cohen before Senate Committee on Commerce, Science, and Transportation, April 5, 1979, p. 5.

[4] Ibid., p. 6.

[5] Leister and Stram, "Vertical Integration."

[6] Testimony of Marvin S. Cohen before Senate Committee on Commerce, Science, and Transportation, April 5, 1979, p. 6.

[7] Statement of Dr. John J. Fearnsides, deputy undersecretary, Department of Transportation, before the Senate Committee on Commerce, Science, and Transportation, April 5, 1979, Appendix B. The 1978 figure is somewhat inflated because of the inclusion of a small number of available ton-miles previously allocated to international all-cargo service.

[8] *Aviation Week*, October 23, 1978. After discontinuance of freighter service at St. Louis by TWA, Tiger added that city to its domestic route system. Statement of Dr. John J. Fearnsides before Senate Committee on Commerce, Science, and Transportation, April 5, 1979, p. 4.

[9] See Chapter 1, above.

portation provided by ICC-licensed carriers under contract.[10] The other two all-cargo carriers have also entered new domestic markets since the passage of the reform legislation: Airlift between Chicago and New York and the Pacific Northwest, and Seaboard between New York and Chicago, Los Angeles, and San Francisco. Before the law was changed, Seaboard had been prevented by the CAB from carrying domestic traffic in or out of New York and as a result had abandoned its domestic services.[11]

The larger commuter cargo carriers have acted on their previous plans to place in operation bigger and more economical equipment, notably the B-727s and Convair 580s for which Federal Express and Summit had been unable to obtain regulatory sanction. Partly as a result of the new aircraft, total shipments handled by Federal Express in 1978 were 38 percent higher than the 1977 level; in 1977 shipments had been only 15 percent in excess of the 1976 figures. For the all-cargo commuters as a group, shipments in 1978 were almost 34 percent above 1977, as compared with a 1976–1977 rise of 29 percent.[12] Although more commuters are expected to put large equipment into operation in the current year, the scarcity and high price of suitable aircraft will constrain their expansion in the near future.[13]

Some cargo service improvements have been inaugurated by the trunkline carriers: for example, as a direct result of the legislation, Pan American has been able to carry domestic freight on U.S. sectors of its international services, and freighter flights operated by United have increased by 20 percent.[14] TWA, however, has abandoned

---

[10] Statement of Wayne M. Hoffman, chairman of the board, Flying Tiger Line, Inc., before the Senate Committee on Commerce, Science, and Transportation, April 5, 1979, p. 6.

[11] Statement of Dr. John J. Fearnsides before Senate Committee on Commerce, Science, and Transportation, April 5, 1979, p. 3. It may be conjectured that Seaboard's new freedom to compete domestically, as well as the apparently permissive general regulatory policy on the part of the present CAB, influenced the decision of Flying Tiger to seek to acquire control of Seaboard.

[12] Testimony of Marvin S. Cohen before Senate Committee on Commerce, Science, and Transportation, April 5, 1979.

[13] Testimony of H. Boyce Budd, Jr., executive vice-president of Summit Airlines and chairman of the board of directors of the Commuter Airline Association of America, before the Senate Committee on Commerce, Science, and Transportation, April 5, 1979, p. 4: "It is estimated that a total of 200 aircraft will be added to the all-cargo fleets of the short-haul carriers over the coming year. All-cargo carriers are buying used Convairs, Electras, DC-6's, DC-8's, and B-707's to expand their cargo services. Because of this demand, the availability of [this class of] aircraft has become very limited, and the price has become very high."

[14] Statement of Dr. John J. Fearnsides before Senate Committee on Commerce, Science, and Transportation, April 5, 1979.

freighter service because its 707 aircraft became impossible to operate profitably at current fuel prices.[15] Among the supplementals, Evergreen International Airlines initiated prime-time scheduled service up and down both East and West Coasts and was considering expansion into interior points.[16] Zantop, a specialist in the charter carriage of automobile parts from Detroit to various destinations, instituted scheduled service from these points to Detroit. In the prereform era, the carrier had of course been limited to charter carriage only and was forced to fly back to Detroit empty when no return charter was available.[17]

In all, seventy-four carriers received all-cargo certificates during the grandfather period. Among these were ten trunklines, three all-cargo carriers, fifty-two air taxis, and nine supplementals.[18] After general open entry became effective in November 1978, twenty-nine new applications were made to the CAB. Most of the new applicants included were freight forwarders and contract carriers; however, a few were newcomers to the air freight business.[19]

In spite of the increase in service, some shippers in mid-1978 were continuing to complain of insufficient freighter capacity and were indicating interest in obtaining charter service through shippers' cooperatives.[20] Emery Air Freight, which had earlier assembled a charter fleet to remedy the shortage of freighter service in the East, began five-day-a-week nighttime air freight service in a north-south direction on the West Coast.[21] Along with other large forwarders, Emery has applied for authority to engage in scheduled direct air carriage. The failure of scheduled air carriers to provide immediately the additional capacity demanded by shippers may readily be explained by the passenger boom and the relative scarcity of suitable equipment. It is to be expected, however, that this scarcity will be ultimately remedied, perhaps after several years. At any rate, the

---

[15] *Wall Street Journal*, November 6, 1978.

[16] *Aviation Week*, November 6, 1978.

[17] Testimony of Marvin S. Cohen before Senate Committee on Commerce, Science, and Transportation, April 5, 1979, pp. 4–5.

[18] Ibid., p. 2.

[19] Presentation of the U.S. Civil Aeronautics Board before the Subcommittee on Aviation, U.S. House Committee on Public Works and Transportation, July 25, 1979, p. 56. Although nineteen of these applications have been awarded, almost all of the contemplated operations are still in the planning stage.

[20] *Journal of Commerce*, July 21, 1978. Shippers' cooperatives, or cooperative shippers' associations, perform a function similar to that of air freight forwarders but are permitted to serve only members of the association. All net earnings of such associations are paid out to the individual members.

[21] *AirCargo Magazine*, October 1978.

shortage cannot be attributed to the reform legislation; reported disillusionment with the measure on the part of some shippers has evidently arisen from unrealistic expectations.

### Changes in Freight Rates and Related Charges to Shippers

Those who expected general price reductions in the present period of inflation were predictably doomed to be disappointed. In addition, since the air freight rate *structure* had not been subjected to rigid regulatory controls that inhibited selective cost-justified price reductions, such reductions have been less widespread and conspicuous as a result of deregulation in the air freight than in the air passenger field.

General freight rate increases have occurred in 1978 and 1979;[22] it seems highly unlikely, however, that the level of air freight rates has been higher since the reform legislation than it would have been without the law. As has been noted, the CAB had pursued no systematic policy which would have prevented freight rates from reflecting experienced cost increases, so that price increases which the CAB considered to be cost-justified would no doubt have been accommodated under regulation. In August 1977 the CAB officially found that an increase of 41.8 percent (as compared with the 1976 level) in the scheduled freight yield for the trunkline and all-cargo carriers was necessary to cover costs.[23] Applying this percentage increase to the 1976 freight yield reported by the CAB results in a "cost-covering" freight yield of 40.57 cents. For the twelve-month period ended September 1978, average freight revenue per ton-mile amounted to 35.6 cents for the domestic trunks and 28.1 cents for the domestic operations of the all-cargo airlines.[24] Therefore, it

---

[22] "Since November 1977, across-the-board increases have occurred in March–April 1978 (10 percent), January–February 1979 (6–15 percent) and again in April–May 1979 (5 percent)." Presentation of the U.S. Civil Aeronautics Board before the House Subcommittee on Aviation, cited in note 19 above, pp. 63–64. Statement of Dr. John J. Fearnsides before Senate Committee on Commerce, Science, and Transportation, p. 5. A study by the CAB has indicated a substantial rise in the average freight rate level between 1977 and 1978. According to this study, a sample of freight shipments carried by certificated airlines in May 1977 would have cost 14 percent more to ship in May 1978. Testimony of Marvin S. Cohen before Senate Committee on Commerce, Science, and Transportation, p. 6.

[23] Civil Aeronautics Board, Order 77-8-62 (1977), p. 42.

[24] Calculated from Civil Aeronautics Board, *Air Carrier Traffic Statistics* and *Air Carrier Financial Statistics*, September 1978. The figure for the all-cargo carriers is subject to correction because of the above-mentioned inclusion of certain international traffic in the domestic traffic statistics. In its July 1979 Presentation

appears that the actual freight rate level was well within the bounds of what would have been permitted under continued regulation, even if costs had remained the same between 1976 and 1978.

Moreover, it seems probable that the reform legislation has encouraged selective rate reductions by making it possible for carriers quickly to raise experimental rates which turn out to be unprofitable. Such selective reductions have been common in the postreform period,[25] and carrier spokesmen have expressed the view that experimental pricing would have been much less likely had the traditional regulatory regime been continued.[26]

On the other hand, traditional regulation apparently would not have permitted increased special charges, such as those which have been put into effect for live animals and hazardous materials, or the changes made in the rules governing liability for "special and consequential" damages[27] and in the standard liability limit, which has been set by some carriers at relatively low levels.

With respect to liability and claims, the CAB had found the existing carrier rules to be unlawful[28] and had prescribed a standard liability limit of $9.07 per pound per piece, as compared with the 50 cent limit per pound per shipment then specified by most carriers. Since regulatory reform, a number of carriers have returned to their old practices in some or all of these categories, and some have acted to increase excess valuation charges from 10–15 cents to 40 cents per

before the House Subcommittee on Aviation, cited in note 19 above, the CAB stated its findings (p. 64) "that overall domestic yield has increased by roughly 10 percent above the rate of inflation between November 1977 and March 1979."

[25] See, for example, the statement of Wayne M. Hoffman before Senate Committee on Commerce, Science, and Transportation, pp. 11–12: "TWA has established new contract belly rates offering discounts to shippers with an agreed volume tender; United has also offered further discounts for high-density daylight traffic intended for carriage in belly service. Frontier and American have published reduced space available belly rates. Eastern has recently introduced new rates for shipper-provided co tainer[s] and multi-containers which, for high-density freight, approach surface freight rate levels . . . just two months ago, Tiger introduced new reduced rates for door-to-door services nationwide which in typical situations decreased the air service price for some direct shippers by 5 to 15 percent. In some cases the reductions were as much as 25 percent. We also introduced a new second day door-to-door eastbound service from California at rates which approximate surface rates for commodities of similar shipping densities."

[26] Aviation Week, April 2, 1979.

[27] Special and consequential damages include extraordinary shipper losses, resulting from carrier actions such as tardy delivery or delivery of goods in a damaged state, but not limited to the intrinsic value of the goods themselves.

[28] Civil Aeronautics Board, Annual Report, 1976.

$100 of excess declared value.[29] In all three respects, however, carrier practice reportedly continues to be nonuniform, as it had been before the CAB's ruling. For example, Flying Tiger retained the $9.07 liability limit as it had done for years before the CAB's decision, and several major carriers did not adopt any increase in the excess valuation charge.

Thus, the experience does not suggest that the deregulated direct air carriers have made a concerted effort to take advantage of the shipper; rather it appears that each airline is constructing its own package of charges and services in accordance with what is perceived to be the needs of its own market. Moreover, the shipper as always has available to him the offers of the air freight forwarders, who may present a more suitable combination of charges and services. At the same time that the CAB declared that, in view of the passage of P.L. 95-163, it would not attempt to enforce its previous decision on liability and claims, a Los Angeles forwarder announced that it had increased its own liability limit from 50 cents to $9.07 per pound.[30]

Similarly, it does not appear that the higher special charges for live animals and hazardous materials represent monopolistic exploitations of the shipper. As the chairman of the CAB has noted, the officially approved level of these special charges had been so low as to give rise to frequent complaints that carriers were not willing to handle these types of freight, and higher charges should result in increased availability of the service.[31]

### Additional Reforms, Accomplished and Proposed

Since the enactment of P.L. 95-163, the CAB has acted to expand the authority of air freight forwarders and shippers' cooperatives[32] and to permit the same company to operate both as an all-cargo certificated carrier and as an exempt commuter.[33] The agency has rejected a proposal to allow direct air carriers to pay commissions to

---

[29] *AirCargo Magazine*, June 1978. These charges are levied to cover the cost of insuring against losses in excess of the standard liability limit.

[30] *AirCargo Magazine*, October 1978.

[31] Alfred E. Kahn, "Air Freight Forwarding in an Era of Regulatory Reform," presentation at the Annual Spring Meeting of the Air Freight Forwarders Association of America, June 2, 1978, pp. 8–9.

[32] Under the new rules, both domestic and international air freight forwarders and also shippers' cooperatives are permitted to use the services of other forwarders, and the cooperatives' authority is extended to transactions involving overseas and foreign air transportation.

[33] Civil Aeronautics Board, ER-1039 (1978).

forwarders on shipments tendered by them[34] but has left open the possibility that the carriers may be allowed to pay the forwarders a "ready-for-carriage" fee which would amount to much the same thing.[35] A major reform initiative has been the CAB's campaign against the ICC's decision in February 1979 to expand the PUD zone by only ten miles—to a thirty-five-mile radius from airports (or boundaries of cities certificated for air service).[36] In its petition for reconsideration of this decision, the CAB has taken the position that no strict mileage limitation should be imposed, but rather a flexible limit which would permit air carriers to perform all surface carriage "incidental to air transportation." Alternatively, the CAB has proposed that, if a mileage limit is to be set, it should be at the one hundred-mile radius originally suggested when the ICC began the proceeding.[37]

Expansion of the PUD zone would facilitate the growth of expedited intermodal freight service by enlarging the area within which surface carriage could be provided by air carriers without ICC restriction. This step would not, however, provide the unrestricted surface authority which would be required to furnish maximum opportunity for the development of such a service. For this sort of authority to become available, a much more far-reaching change in motor carrier regulatory policy would be necessary.

## New Regulations Governing Air Freight Forwarders and Direct Air Cargo Carriers

On November 8, 1978, the CAB adopted permanent regulations governing domestic air cargo transportation under the new law, and in January 1979 a similar set of new regulations[38] was adopted for indirect air carriers. The new regulations for direct air cargo transportation appear for the most part to be consistent with the intent of the law and justified by the more competitive conditions which the statute creates. Thus, the simplified reporting requirements, the removal of the necessity to establish and justify reasonable rates, the exemption of intercarrier transactions such as mergers and agree-

---

[34] Civil Aeronautics Board, EDR-330 (1978).

[35] *AirCargo Magazine*, March 1979.

[36] Ibid. It should be noted, however, that the new regulation redefines the boundaries from which the radius is computed in such a way that, in some instances, the zone could be more than twice as large as before.

[37] *Traffic World*, February 26, 1979.

[38] Civil Aeronautics Board, ER-1080, and ER-1094.

ments from CAB control (which has involved immunity from prosecution under the antitrust laws), and the more stringent requirements regarding the maintenance of public liability insurance all reflect the new freedom of the industry from protective regulation. (Transactions between major air cargo carriers are still subject to the existing CAB jurisdiction, however, because these carriers are also engaged in international air cargo transportation and/or air passenger transportation, neither of which is covered by the regulation.) The most controversial features of the new regime are the elimination of the tariff-filing requirement and of the duty to furnish transportation upon reasonable request, both of which are now being challenged in the courts.[39]

An even more liberal regime was adopted with respect to indirect air carriers (that is, air freight forwarders and cooperative shippers' associations). Describing the new framework to a meeting of air freight forwarders, the chairman of the CAB noted that it would serve:

> to make entry into the industry almost totally free, to get us out of the business of certifying fitness, and reducing entrance requirements to the bare minimum of identification; to eliminate most of the operating restrictions on indirect air carriers; exempt you from having to file tariffs; eliminate practically all the reporting requirements to which you are now subject; and to eliminate the Board's control over who owns you, serves on your boards, or whom you own, or with whom you are or may be affiliated. The only consumer protection [retained under the new regime] is over the kind of insurance you carry, and the information you provide shippers about your insurance and liability limits, because here is where we are not satisfied complete decontrol and a total reliance on the principle of let the buyer beware will suffice.[40]

In view of the very liberal regulatory control exercised over forwarders by the CAB in the past, these changes are by no means as revolutionary as they might appear. For forwarders, entry control has been of practically negligible significance, as has control over the level of rates. In this case also, the most controversial element is the

---

[39] *National Small Shipments Traffic Conference and Drug and Toilet Preparation Traffic Conference, et al. v. CAB*, CADC Case Nos. 78-2163, 78-2164. The U.S. Court of Appeals for the District of Columbia circuit has denied the petitioners' motion for a stay of these exemptions pending review.

[40] Kahn, "Air Freight Forwarding," p. 3.

exemption from the requirement that tariffs be filed and adhered to, an exemption which was unanimously opposed by shippers as well as major carrier representatives.[41]

The issues involved in the tariff-filing dispute will not be explored in depth here. However, the disposition of this issue obviously has important implications for the future course of regulation in the air and surface freight fields and, possibly, in the field of air passenger transportation. Whatever the courts may decide regarding the legality of the CAB's action,[42] future policy will most likely be decided by actual experience under the new framework. The CAB has acted in the belief that legal sanctions are not necessary to provide essential advance information to shippers or to protect them from discrimination, and it has in fact predicted that publication of rates and rules will continue in much the same fashion as before, with faithful adherence to tariffs in spite of the lack of a legal requirement.[43] If experience bears out this belief, Congress may well decide to allow the present policy to continue even though, arguably, its adoption may have been contrary to the intent of the existing law.

### The Postreform Experience: Overview and Prospects

The foregoing preliminary survey of the early postreform experience has shown that there have been important improvements in air cargo transportation service and some cost reductions, which could not

---

[41] In EDR-359 (1978), at p. 6, the CAB succinctly described the reaction to its proposal to abolish the tariff-filing requirement for forwarders: "Not only carriers, but shippers' traffic departments as well, unanimously oppose it."

[42] In this connection, the statement on tariff-filing in the conference report on H.R. 6010 is obviously of very great significance. See Chapter 2, above.

[43] Civil Aeronautics Board, ER-1094, p. 3: "The Board has never doubted the value to the shipper of the rate and rule information contained in the tariffs. In reviewing the comments in this case and observing how the present air cargo system works, including the practices of air taxis without tariffs, the Board has concluded that there are sufficient economic incentives to ensure that this flow of information to the shipper will continue. Here also, the forwarders will continue to publish their own rate sheets and service guides, as they do now, and will continue to make them readily available to the shipping public. In fact the forwarders can, and undoubtedly will, continue to construct and distribute their rates as they do now through an independent publisher, but without the need to conform to government-imposed guidelines. A forwarder's ability to successfully market its services depends to a large extent on *informing the public of its charges and in abiding by them.*" (Emphasis supplied.) Under the new regime, the industry's long-standing practice of publishing (through the Airline Tariff Publishing Company) a comprehensive listing of all carriers' cargo rates every fifteen days has in fact continued.

have taken place without regulatory reform, and that further improvements may be expected in the near future. Simultaneously, the traffic, revenues, and profits of the certificated carriers have continued to increase; there has obviously been no "wholesale loss of air service and loss of employment to thousands of skilled career airline employees."[44] The price structure has become more complex and more reflective of the costs of particular kinds of service, and there is no evidence that the price level has been higher than it would have been if the previous regulatory scheme had remained in effect. The prospects for additional service improvements have been enhanced by several CAB actions that have further liberalized the regulatory framework, but opportunities for maximum development of an expedited, intermodal freight service remain inhibited by regulations affecting the provision of surface carriage.[45] Development of this service would require not only expansion of the PUD zone in the manner suggested by the CAB, but also permission for direct and indirect air carriers to supply surface transportation for freight not having a prior or subsequent movement by aircraft. As Wayne M. Hoffman has pointed out, not only has the air cargo reform law fallen far short of removing unnecessary restriction on integrated intermodal operations, but it has also put air carriers at an unjustified disadvantage vis-à-vis surface carriers in developing such operations.[46]

With the possible exception of the elimination of the tariff-filing requirement and of the duty to transport upon reasonable request, the postreform CAB-initiated changes in the regulation of air freight forwarders and direct air cargo carriers appear to be of relatively little practical significance. Because of the strong protests of some shipper groups,[47] the possibility exists that tariff-filing, pre-

---

[44] See Chapter 2, note 22 above.

[45] See Clinton H. Whitehurst, Jr., ed., *Forming Multimodal Transportation Companies* (Washington, D.C.: American Enterprise Institute, 1979).

[46] Statement of Wayne M. Hoffman before Senate Committee on Commerce, Science, and Transportation, April 5, 1979, pp. 16–17. As Hoffman states, "it is now possible without significant regulatory interference or expense for a direct or indirect surface carrier to obtain air freight transportation authority and thus provide integrated intermodal services on a nationwide basis. . . . There is, however, no practical way in which an all-cargo air carrier can obtain comparable nationwide direct or indirect surface authority from the ICC. . . . The result is to subject any air carrier seeking authority to provide intermodal services to the complex and costly passage by protest through the ICC regulatory maze."

[47] See, for example, the testimony of William J. Wilds III on behalf of the Society of American Florists, and William J. Augello, executive director/general counsel, Shippers National Freight Claim Council, Inc., before the U.S. Senate Committee on Commerce, Science, and Transportation, April 5, 1979.

scribed carrier liability provisions, and the duty to furnish transportation upon reasonable request will be the subject of further congressional action. Regardless of future judicial findings concerning the legality of the CAB's exemptions, it appears that actual experience under the new regime will ultimately determine regulatory policy on these issues.

# 4

# Summary and Conclusion

## A Synopsis

Although the imposing array of regulatory controls over the air cargo industry did not prevent its persistent growth and development, including the initiation of all-cargo airlines and innovative small-plane air freight services (both of which achieved a foothold in the industry by taking advantage of existing regulatory exemptions from the ordinary requirement for certification), these controls did produce certain seriously undesirable economic effects. Thus, the quality of service offered to shippers of air freight in important domestic markets deteriorated greatly in the years preceding the enactment of the reform legislation, and this deterioration would not have been possible in the absence of protective entry control. Controls over operating authority also gave rise to small cost increases which could have grown to more significant proportions if they had been allowed to continue. Limitations on the surface transportation authority available to air carriers raised—and continue to raise—unnecessary obstacles to broader experimentation in high-quality intermodal freight service.

With regard to price control, the evidence does not seem to indicate that minimum rate regulation has caused underutilization of belly space in combination aircraft. Nor has maximum rate regulation, in most of the period under review, hampered the development of freight service in all-cargo aircraft by setting rate ceilings generally inadequate for cost coverage. Controlled entry, however, may have helped to bring about higher rates for belly freight transportation by obstructing the supply of the substitute (freighter) service and thus producing a less elastic demand for belly freight transportation. Moreover, the ever present possibility that public utility–type rate control might cause adverse effects by preventing prompt price increases in response to inflationary cost rises apparently became a reality when fuel costs exploded a few years ago. And the requirement that air carriers charge ICC-determined motor carrier rates for surface carriage outside the PUD zone limited the development of expedited intermodal freight transportation.

The impact of the undesirable effects of the prereform regime was felt not only by shippers but also by those producers of freight transportation, including direct and indirect carriers, whose opportunities to provide more—and better—service were circumscribed by regulation. Their representatives became persuasive advocates of liberalization, in marked contrast to the conventional obstructionism of the majority of the spokesmen for the combination carriers during most of the debate on airline regulatory reform. As shown in Chapter 3, the support of direct and indirect carriers was one important factor in bringing about the early enactment of genuine reform—not only because of the strength of their economic case but probably also because it was presented by individuals with first-hand experience who would be directly affected by the proposed legislation. Evidence of direct participants seems almost always (and perhaps often rightly) to carry more weight in Congress than the views of those whose interest is prompted by more general considerations of "public welfare." Their persuasiveness was enhanced by their willingness to accept change on a much larger scale than would have been necessary to solve their own particular problems. It seems unlikely, however, that industry representatives would have originated a broad-scale reform proposal on their own initiative, if only because such a proposal would have seemed less likely to succeed than some more limited regulatory measure. Therefore, the ready availability of a broad reform proposal with the support of the CAB and the administration was also, it appears, a necessary factor in the process. Also crucial to the prompt achievement of reform was enlightened and effective congressional leadership. During the nineteen-month progress of the legislation from the CAB's proposal to presidential signature, the major changes that took place were all in a liberalizing direction, and efforts to create privileged positions for certain narrow producer groups were uniformly defeated.

The early postreform experience has demonstrated that expectations of more, better, and more efficient freight service were fully justified, and there seems little reason to fear a return to a more protective regulatory regime. Those who have felt the impact of the new competition authorized by the reform law have nevertheless grown and prospered. The early success and acceptance of the law suggests that regulatory roadblocks will not again permit service deterioration and obstruct the efficient provision of innovative forms of air freight transportation, that price rises needed to cover inflationary cost increases will not be blocked, and that pricing straitjackets, such as were proposed by the administrative law judge in the Domestic Air Freight Rate Investigation,[1] will not serve to reduce the utilization of air freight carrying capacity (although vigilance will be needed to prevent antidiscrimination regulation from developing a tendency in this direction). Moreover, the absence of control over rate "reasonableness" promotes experimentation with lower prices undeterred by any prospective difficulty of raising rates which turn out to have been set uneconomically low. In addition, it may be predicted with some confidence that more attention will be given to the permanent legal framework within which the deregulated industry is to operate. More conjectural is the possibility that the momentum of air cargo reform will facilitate further liberalization of the regulation of surface carriage provided by air carriers in conjunction with or in substitution for air transportation.

## A Lesson for the Future?

There seems to be a lesson in this experience for advocates of economic regulatory reform in other fields. Liberalizing regulation may in many instances provide important benefits, such as opportunities for service improvements and cost reductions, which accrue in part to the producer interests involved as well as to the consumers, and identification of and emphasis on these benefits can be effective in gaining broad support. This sort of opportunity exists in the field of surface carriage and is also apparently exemplified in the recent experience with air passenger transportation, where liberalized price regulation brought large gains to carriers and users alike.

Most of the industry strongly opposed regulatory reform of passenger transportation, although some large combination carriers—which stood to gain from the opportunity to enter new markets denied to them under the existing regulatory scheme—were relatively early supporters of liberalization. The attitude of the majority of the airlines did not change until the CAB, on its own initiative, adopted in the latter part of 1977 a much less restrictive policy toward carrier pricing than had been followed in the immediately preceding years.

---

[1] Civil Aeronautics Board, *Domestic Air Freight Rate Investigation*, Docket 22859, Initial Decision of the Administrative Law Judge (1975).

After this policy switch, certain carriers quickly took advantage of the opportunity to institute promotional pricing, and others who had been skeptical of the wisdom of such a course were compelled, for competitive reasons, to follow suit. Although the ensuing spectacular increase in traffic—accompanied by more intensive utilization of equipment and other facilities—was partially attributable to the general rise in national prosperity, there is little doubt that the new pricing strategies were largely responsible. There was, indeed, a small reduction in the average passenger fare (as measured by average revenue per passenger-mile), but the profits of the airlines increased substantially. (In real terms, the average fare declined significantly.) At the same time, of course, the general public became much more aware of the general benefits arising from decontrol. Industry support for reform gained momentum throughout 1978, and in the fall the Airline Deregulation Act of 1978[2] passed with few dissenting voices.

At present it seems unlikely that administrative action will initiate on a comparable scale the same sort of "preview" demonstration of the benefits of decontrol in the field of surface transportation. However, there appear to be important opportunities here for cost reductions and service improvements, the gains from which would accrue to producer and consumer interests alike. It would undoubtedly be worthwhile, in connection with current proposals for decontrol of surface transportation, to call renewed attention to these opportunities.

In fact, the railroad industry seems already to have appreciated these opportunities and, accordingly, has altered its attitude toward reform. Regulatory controls over the rail price level and structure have had obviously deleterious effects on railroad finances and on the quality of service offered to the public. Both shippers in general and carrier interests have suffered from regulatory restrictions on the abandonment of unprofitable branch lines serving relatively minor shipper groups. Overall rail employment has probably also been adversely affected.

Similarly, persuasive evidence indicates that potential cost reductions and service improvements in trucking are systematically blocked by ICC regulation of rates and operating authority.[3] For example, the rigid system of prescribed class rates prevents truckers from offering the price-service options desired by various types of shipper. Both

---

[2] U.S. Congress, P.L. 95-504, 95th Congress, 2d Session, October 24, 1978.

[3] See, for example, John W. Snow, "The Problem of Motor Carrier Regulation and the Ford Administration's Proposal for Reform," in *Regulation of Entry and Pricing in Truck Transportation*, ed. Paul W. MacAvoy and John W. Snow (Washington, D.C.: American Enterprise Institute, 1977).

those who would prefer better service at a higher price and those who would like to pay less and receive lower-quality (for example, less speedy) service cannot be accommodated at the standard price. In many cases, these unsatisfied demands are diverted to private carriage. Restrictions on differential backhaul pricing, which limit the use of trucks on return trips, and restrictions on off-peak pricing, which prevent motor carriers from offering truly cost-based rates, limit utilization of equipment and other facilities and thus increase average costs and prices. Controls over operating authority effectively limit the range of commodities that individual carriers may handle, as well as the routes which they may serve, and thus obviously limit equipment utilization. Controls over the routes served often result in unnecessary truck mileage and excessive interlining (transfers from one trucking firm to another), both of which inflate costs and lower the quality of the service.

Among the major beneficiaries from the removal of these types of control would be the common carriers of general freight—especially those who serve the less-than-truckload market—who would lose their regulation-induced competitive disadvantage in relation to private carriage. Specialized carriers would also benefit from the broadening of their available markets. Both of these groups would, of course, become more exposed to new competition than they are at present; whether the new opportunities would be valued more highly than the lost security remains an open question. Nevertheless, as the air cargo experience has shown, these opportunities can form the basis for an important and powerful part of the case for regulatory reform.